eLearning THEORIES & DESIGNS

Between Theory & Practice.
A Guide For Novice Instructional Designers

AWATEF BOULEDROUA

PARTRIDGE

Library of Congress Control Number: 2021900235
ISBN: Hardcover   978-1-5437-6291-4
                   Softcover   978-1-5437-6290-7
                   eBook   978-1-5437-6292-1

To order additional copies of this book, contact
Toll Free +65 3165 7531 (Singapore)
Toll Free +60 3 3099 4412 (Malaysia)
orders.singapore@partridgepublishing.com

www.partridgepublishing.com/singapore

CONTENTS

PREFACE

The present book is a collection of information considered useful for junior instructional designers who aim to build a strong instructional design. It decorticates the theories of learning and how they are reflected in the different practices by creating effective designs and instructions with diversified teaching methods and tools.

The book is designed to guide new instructional designers who wish to understand the pillars that will lead them in creating balanced eLearning content based on learning theories and the current technologies in reshaping the learning effectively.

The idea of compiling a book from previous separate articles and assignments came from a self-reflective process on the learning journey I had at Hamdan Bin Mohammed Smart University, Dubai (UAE). During this journey, I faced many challenges that shaped my learning experience in instructional design thanks to the knowledgeable professors I had the honor been their student while preparing for a master's degree in e-education curriculum and instruction.

The amount of information I exposed myself to during this learning process and the diversity of content I could read and explore made this book possible in many ways: the interest I found myself nurturing in instructional design and the resources, updated information, and the multitude of social media I follow in this field where people talk about their challenges and the tools they use as designers, the problems they face, and how they solve complicated situations, especially in the time of COVID-19, gave me powerful knowledge that I gather here as an artifact of my learning during these years.

INTRODUCTION

With the advent of technology, the use of learning theories was superficial and unstable. This fact made learning designs weak and incompatible with the teaching and learning requirements of technology, flexibility, and engagement.

According to Reynolds and Mason (2016), eLearning started as a weak learning implementation and was less than satisfying for both schools and universities. In the beginning, the problem resided in the involved parts of the learning process: the educators, the learners, and the developers of software and applications who were new in creating effective learning with technology.

On one hand, the educators were using technology as a resource of information and could not apply the acquired learning theories on their instructions easily. On the other hand, there was the learner, disrupted by the abundance of resources, could not recognize the good from the bad resources, and collecting knowledge was unsuccessful most of the time because of the lack of guidance from the educators, which made this resource-rich tool that we call the internet a waste of time for both learners and educators. And last, we have the developers who were not focusing on education while they were designing applications and software. Therefore, most technological contents provided for learning were not completely made to create balanced educational resources; they were mostly game-based learning.

Later, learning objectives were included in the instructional process and design of education. Learning objectives were included in each technological content, showing the accommodation of the application and what is exactly the learning outcome that is targeted to empower learning. In parallel, learners, educators, and software developers had a focus on how people learn using several learning theories and building their instruction on data collected from User Experience (UX). The content came out more educational, better organized, and well-structured for teaching and learning purposes.

Now, the role of the instructional designers is to create resources and platforms to incorporate learning with/from technology at its best and to avoid shallow content and resources that do not target a specific learning outcome. They also try to accommodate their content to engage the learners, not in using technology to learn but to create learning techniques that enhance the outcome and illustrate the growth of the learner in manipulating technology as well. Learning theories are the roadmap for every instructional designer who aims to build structured, engaging, and flexible learning with technology.

The future of learning and technology will create new perspectives that few have an idea of how it will develop and how it will increase the perception of the learners. How an instructional designer can apply learning theories created from the time of the Second World War for military purposes (Edgar, 2012) to sustain learning with a futuristic technology that has new dimensions? Are we going to experience the creation of new theories like connectivism that was created to understand learning in the digital age and be able to regulate our new theories or learning to suit the new era that is not known yet? Are we going to shift our focus from the learner's needs and wants to the machine thinking? These questions will not be answered in this book, but the book itself represents an introduction to the paradigm shift we're expecting in eLearning.

In these chapters, the known learning theories are highlighted to explain how an instructional designer could shift his programs and courses into eLearning in this pandemic and build constructivist eLearning environments. We will try to understand many aspects of learning theories and their application in contemporary environments of eLearning. We will also conclude this journey and try to speculate the future of these aspects in an imaginary learning environment.

CHAPTER I
LEARNING THEORIES

TERMINOLOGY

Many new terminologies emerged from the educational field, and the existing ones included other definitions when integrated in eLearning practices. That is why a need to elaborate on the terminology of some words is necessary before we dig into the eLearning field and describe its theories, practices, and designs.

First of all, we need to explain the following terminology according to online usage and practices. This terminology is used in this book according to its main meaning in eLearning applications.

Approach: According to the English Language Learners Definition of approach (Entry 2 of 2): approach is a way of dealing with something, a way of doing or thinking about something. It is how to deal with a problem or a situation. In learning, approaches are not theories; they are the way that we prefer to use in certain situations and that we think is the best way to cover it. For example, I prefer to embrace in my instructional design a *self-paced approach*, as it allows my learners to master the skills at their own pace and time.

Instructor: In this book, the instructor is the main individual who guides the learners, provides the learning material, and gives feedback to the learners.

Blended Learning: It is a learning situation where two or more combinations of learning formats can take place: it can be classroom-based learning combined with online learning or asynchronous combined with synchronous fully online learning, or any other combination that allows the student to learn in two different places, times, or situations.

Course Content: The content represents the resources needed to present the lesson or the topic or the subject to learn.

Course Structure: The structure is how your course is sequenced and presented. It is about the organization and the display of the content in the platform. The structure should support the learning modules and objectives of the course.

Learning Format: Formats in eLearning may vary between synchronous and asynchronous classes, online and face-to-face sessions.

Time Zone: Timing is a crucial element in online learning, as the learners might have a different time zone. If the platform used in eLearning does not show the time of the students' zone, then the time is set at the instructor's time zone per default.

Study Weeks: Online learning is counted per "week of study." It can be six, eight, or fifteen weeks long whether for one school term (which is usually twelve to fifteen weeks per term) or college terms.

LEARNING THEORIES IN PRACTICE

Learning theories are the guidelines that any instructional designer needs to accomplish his instruction effectively, but how can we implement them in a way that makes the learning experience balanced and well-structured for the learners with effective learning outcomes.

Before we start, we need to understand the difference between effective and efficient. Are we looking for an effective eLearning or an efficient eLearning?

Well, *effective* learning is to create the right learning for your students, taking into consideration what they want, and using all possible means to accomplish your task. It might take time, expenses, and much effort from the designer and the stakeholder; but the aim is to reach the goals no matter what it takes.

Efficient learning is doing things right; it is about the *how* of the instruction: how we are going to reach these goals? Usually, the cost and the effort is accounted for the accomplishment of the task. Being efficient means that the instructional designer is required to explain his expenses and keep them reasonable. In the same time, efficient means to have a learning outcome that is valuable for now and for later, as this will prevent the institution from deploying new expenses.

Now, let's ask the question again: Are we looking to achieve effective learning or efficient learning? I believe effective is more adequate to explain the strategies taken in this book. The instruction and programs we are trying to create will require much time and effort than just reaching goals and building instruction.

The designer can create a new version of an existing instruction or construct new and effective (reaching the goal with all that it takes) eLearning and design programs to give the student an adventure instead of a regular learning experience.

At this point, we need to understand the importance of learning theories for the instructional designer and to emphasize how much learning theories can improve the assimilation of the content that needs to be delivered to the learners.

An overview will be provided to the reader to summarize the need of learning theories in an instructional design process. We will include two basic views on the topic. One will be conducted on the pedagogical approach (classroom learning), and the second will be applied to the andragogical approach (adult learning).

The study will include examples of how theories of learning are used in instructional design (ID) and how the knowledge concepts (psychology, communication, and technology) are approached using the theories of learning: behaviorism, cognitivism, social learning, and self-directed and transformative learning theories. Then, we will highlight the most effective ID model we selected among the five models known, and we will explain how the instructional designer can choose the most appropriate and effective ID according to the goals to achieve.

In addition to that, theories of learning are used in eLearning platforms to design a balanced learning experience: *Behaviorism* is used mostly to include the rewarding and instant feedback that are major elements in motivating the learners. *Social learning theory* is used for observation especially at the beginning of the instruction, by including videos and simulations to shift the learner toward the right behavior. *Cognitivism* is mostly covering the systematic tests and assessments that these platforms are usually providing to the learner to measure how much he is learning and to keep him informed about the highlights of the course. *Constructivism* is the key theory for the online learning platforms where the student is watched in how he constructs and builds his learning while interacting with others. In these smart environments, students are usually conducting self-paced learning. With *constructivism*, many theories emerged like the *transformational learning theory*, which consists of self-reflection and student-centered learning. Also, the *self-directed learning theory* is important for the student to gain self-efficacy and to define the goals of his learning.

We cannot decide which the most efficient theory for smart learning platforms is, as these are conducted according to the learners' needs, and learning activities are drawn from many theories of learning to cover all learner's knowledge concepts: psychology, communication, and technology.

1. Incorporating Learning Theories

Instructional design is the process of combining several elements to match the learning objectives and goals of the stakeholder to achieve a training or a program in a consistent way.

According to Gary et al. (2012), these factors are important in building effective learning, and they are

- ○ analyzing the learning requirements of the learner,
- ○ measuring the conditions of learning, and

6

o making learning materials and requirements compatible with the theories of learning.

Let's explain these points: It is obvious that the instructional designer has to know first his students and classify his work in two different learning approaches: *Pedagogical approach* to study the instructional design needed and theories for a classroom setting, and *andragogical approach*, where the students are self-paced learners and need another approach with different theories of learning to design a good instruction especially when we talk about eLearning. In the latter, the student is self-directed and is following andragogy more than pedagogy as learning approaches.

Andragogy is a science that refers to adult learning (Kearsley, 2010). In this book, when we consider andragogy as an approach for designing, it allows the instructional designer to integrate andragogical situations for learning and apply them on children learning as we are moving our designs from teacher-centered to student-centered learning. These approaches can give to the design flexibility of adult learning in many ways to cover the self-pacing that we aim to incorporate in most of our instructions.

Self-learning is a facet of futuristic formal and informal learning, and children might be dragged into online learning that considers self-learning as a prerequisite skill to learn. That is why we are trying to shift our learning paradigm gradually into fully online learning where the instructor's role is equivalent to his role in angdragogy.

Learner analysis is what we start with to effectively know our learners and how they learn best. Learner analysis can guide us during the steps in collecting the resources, finding the right way to present the course, to display it, to organize it, and to define the language to be used, the different levels needed for the training or the course, and the technology that is easy to find and use by these particular learners.

Then to measure the conditions of learning, we might use needs assessment to be able to analyse the situation and plan for the instruction. In this book, we will apply a needs assessment and give you a specific situation in which we will explain how you can conduct your needs assessment and what the steps you can go through as part of the planning and analysis phase of the instructional design.

But first, we will try to explain the use of learning theories when we decide to plan for an instruction and how to gather the right information to compile the right set of theories. Once we decide on the theories we need, we can gather our resources and technology that best serve the objectives of the learning.

2. Key Concepts and Principles of ID

The key concepts of instructional design are the important elements that help in building strong learning with better assimilation to achieve the objectives set by the stakeholder.

When a designer decides to build a learning course for certain learners, he must draw theories from several knowledge and science concepts (Seels and Glasgow, 1998):

- o Psychology (behaviorism)
- o Communication (social learning and constructivism)
- o Technology (transformative and self-directed theory)

Each knowledge concept will help in communicating the message in a meaningful manner to the learner.

Traditionally, the instructional design is drawing its theories from *behaviorism* and *cognitivism* (Skinner, Ausubel, and Bruner), and later on, *constructivism* is shown at the surface to watch how people learn by constructing their learning from their experiences and beliefs (Jonassen, 1991). However, the approaches for learning can also contribute to shaping a better learning experience, especially when the instructor tries to blend several approaches to create a new learning design.

Two main approaches to learning are followed: *Pedagogy* and *Andragogy*. Each approach will demonstrate how the instructional designer can construct his design using different strategies to deliver different objectives and goals.

3. Pedagogical Approach

In the pedagogical setting, teachers have predetermined subjects and learning objectives to be delivered within a classroom setting for students receiving learning from their instructor directly. In this learning approach, time is limited for the course delivery, and students need more behavioral learning approaches to keep them involved in the learning process.

In this approach, to deliver meaningful content to the learner (Gary et al., 2012), the instructional designer will use mostly the following:

- o *Behaviorism* (associated with Skinner and Pavlov)
- o *Social learning* (associated with Bandura)
- o *Cognitivism* (associated with Piaget)

The instructional designer will use behaviorism to create outcomes of learning that are measurable and predictable. It helps create reinforcement and rewarding system to control the learning process of the student and his behaviors, to manage the classroom in general and to guide the students during the acquisition of skills and the content to learn.

Behaviorism is used by the instructional designer to guide the learner to what he needs to know and what skills to gain through the memorization of repeated information to get a predictable learning outcome. At the same time, the instructor will guide the student through the usage of reinforcements and feedback to indicate the correct answer or to redirect the student to the right behavior.

Behaviorism, in our daily activities, is based on classical and operant conditioning where stimuli are strong factors to influence human behavior. It is important to understand the benefit we achieve from creating stimuli to control the desired behavior, while punishment is used to discourage the recurrence of some unwanted behaviors. However, sometimes we create a stimulus unconsciously: A mom who calls her children for lunch every day at noon is a stimulus. How? Well, if she calls for lunch at 11:00 a.m., the kids will come to eat anyway, feeling hungry as much as they are used to come at noon. Not one of them will check the time just because their hunger is connected to a stimulus, "the mom's call," not to a specific time.

Social learning theory is a part of behaviorism, but it is connected to the *social learning* based on Bandura's experiences on how people learn from observation and modeling (from others). This allows the student to learn through his environment and by observing the actions of the people around him (Bandura, 1977).

An instructional designer can include videos and learning strategies based on modeling to show to the learner how he is supposed to act when facing the same situation or problem or to highlight the steps to follow or even to use examples based on the modeling learning strategy (Van Gog and Rummel, 2010), and sometimes the design will need to include an activity or a certain learning situation where a peer is a model for a behavior to allow the student to copy his peer and gain the required skill.

At this stage, collaboration can be included in a class setting or in the eLearning platform to perform social learning at its most using social network. We will elaborate on this topic and give practice-based situations to understand the effect of social networking in eLearning.

Cognitivism is a learning theory that focuses on the process of learning happening at the brain instead of the observation of the learner's behavior. The learner is not considered a container anymore who receives knowledge from the teacher directly. The processing of knowledge is focused now on using different strategies.

These strategies, once understood, can be used to enhance the design and create active learning (Ausubel, 1978). The key elements of using cognitivism in instructional design can be summarized in Gagné's model.

Gagné's Nine Events are used to perform better retention of the content and involve the learner by providing him the goals and objectives of his learning before starting the activity.

The instructional designer can use some or all these steps for an effective design, like to recall first the prior knowledge of the learner for the topic as an introduction to the new knowledge.

This step prepares the learner effectively to enhance involvement and motivation and stimulate understanding. Also, the use of strategic organizers can provide helpful guidance and better understanding in practice, like to use organizers in learning languages to give details about the characters in a story. The designer can also use mind-mapping tools and invite the student to demonstrate his learning abilities by reflecting on the activity or summarize and regenerate his understanding in another way like by drawing a concept map (Mento, Martinelli, and Jones, 1999).

4. Andragogical Approach

Andragogy is about adult learning and how to teach professional learners in a self-paced and student-centered environment. This approach uses different learning strategies, as the learner itself is better motivated and free of any obligations to learn. Andragogy is the *"art and science of helping adults learn"* (Knowles, 1980, p. 43).

The learning goal of the adult comes from his own environment, his job, and his intrinsic need to learn. That is why different theories are used in andragogy to conduct effective learning sessions like the *self-directed theory* of learning and *Mazirow's transformational theory* of learning.

In addition to these theories, andragogy for eLearning also requires more theories that we elaborated above under the pedagogical approach for learning—*behaviorism, cognitivism,* and *social learning*— to cover other instructional properties like using feedback, reinforcers, rewards with behaviorism, and inviting the student to learn from his environment by observing others and his peers with *social learning theory.*

Cognitivism is indeed highly recommended in andragogy to measure the learning outcomes and to engage the learner by inviting his attention for active participation (Allen, 2007). It emphasizes the acquisition, processing, and assimilation of knowledge.

The best way to engage the students using cognitivism is to stimulate their thinking and processing of the information by giving activities that help them recognize where they get it wrong and why. In eLearning, these steps can be made first by stimulating their schema, which is connecting their prior knowledge to the new given information. Usually, stimulation in online learning is based on visual and audio stimulators like using vignettes, short videos showing a problem or a situation, or audios and pictures referring to something we need them to recall.

Cognitivists believe that learning leads to activity, while constructivists believe that the activity leads to learning (Jonassen and Rohrer-Murphy, 1999).

However, the main focus while preparing an instructional design for adults is based on the constructivist theory for learning and transformative theory, while the connectivist theory is mainly considered for smart learning environments created to explain how people can learn with social media. This theory is meant for an informal learning setting where people can follow the information they want to know to enrich their knowledge on a specific domain. Resources can vary from what they find, and their findings are not considered for scientific research or to build an academic profile.

a. Self-directed Learning Theory

Andragogy is seen as an independent process where the adult learner keeps track of his learning and builds up his understanding according to what he needs to know and how he needs the knowledge to be mastered (Knowles, 1975). This independent learning is not free from material and resources that an instructor should provide.

Self-learning can be geared by the instructor according to the needs of the student by providing the resources and the material offline and online and to guide him during his journey through several follow-up and discussions (Merriam, 2001). This guidance needs instructional design strategies to be effective, especially when the learner is having problems in shifting to a self-directed learner.

To have an effective learning design with self-directed learners, the instructional designer must

- guide the learners to take decisions on what they want to learn (set the goal and plan for the learning);
- provide resources and materials to help gain the skills (learn) and the competencies the learner needs to achieve the goals;
- determine what the skills gained are to be able to assess accordingly (show); and
- engage the students in self-reflection and self-evaluation by seeking and giving feedback (peer feedback included) to end the learning design with (reflect). It shows to the instructor the skills gained and the performance level of the student.

b. Mezirow's Transformative Theory

This theory is made to explain how adult learners can make sense of their learning using challenges, critical thinking, and questioning to understand their judgments about the world and to construct the new meaning of it (Mezirow, 1991). The process of using this theory to activate effective learning is to plan, act, observe, analyze, reflect, and evaluate.

The application of this theory will focus on the reflective process. Learning will then be made by transforming the schemes of the learners in the virtual communities where a new experience is implemented.

Transformative learning theory is usually focusing on post-secondary education (Taylor, 2007). It is applied to evaluate the level of achievement and the quality of reflection provided by the learner or to measure the self-efficacy of the student in accepting the new changes and know-how to learn from their experiences. It is mainly used in online learning platforms for evaluation and assessment, like to introduce an assessment test at the beginning of the lesson to know exactly where the student stands for the course material. Then, the designer must take into consideration the student experience while posting activities to relate the content to the learner, involve him in a way that makes him define what he needs to know, and give him a chance to link his new learning to his life experiences like to use real situations for problem-solving activities.

c. Social Cognitive Theory: Using Rewards to Motivate Learning

Garaus et al. (2016) have made primary research where they based their work on evidence and statistics to demonstrate the role of rewarding in education. We all know that children react easily when rewarded and can change their behaviors accordingly, but what about undergraduate students in human resource management pursuing online learning?

The pilot study is showing the outcomes and stated results with interesting numbers. This meticulous study has applied comparability of variables, which is a sign of exactitude in statistics and thus in the results. It emphasizes the rewarded behavior according to the social cognitive theory of Bandura (1986). The results were measured according to the change in behavior of the students throughout the study regarding their self- motivation. Two groups of undergraduate students were given online tasks and assignments. Both groups were assessed in a controlled learning environment (a classroom), then in an autonomous learning environment (online learning). The rewarding behavior was measured according to the number of students who accomplished their tasks in controlled learning versus the number of students who did in autonomous learning.

The booster of this study was the rewarding effect on both groups in both environments. As a result, the performance ratio of the rewarded tasks in online learning was eight times higher than the unrewarded tasks ratio even if they were just bonus points on each task.

The study focused also on the outcomes of eLearning with small rewards and the engagement of the students: the findings explain that the small rewarding cannot be considered as the foundation of the autonomous motivation to learn, but it improves it.

Finally, and according to this research, the quantity of tasks achieved is approximately four times higher than those achieved in unrewarded tasks. In other words, students could achieve more tasks when they were rewarded.

5. Adult Learning

Under this title, we will try to understand how theories of learning are reflected in the online communities of practice (CoPs), and to be able to elaborate this point clearly, we will look closer to one of the most known communities of practice at this time on social media called Udemy. By decorticating the different elements of this platform, we will try to understand how learning theories were activated in this platform and explain how much such communities can be beneficial for adult students and instructors.

This shift of paradigm in students' learning from *instructivist theory* to a *constructivist theory* in online paid platforms is a huge step in informal eLearning where adult learners choose to pay for online individual courses than to attend classes in an institute.

In the same perspective of the paradigm shift, we will discuss how novice instructors learn from the community to explore new facets of online learning and cope with sophisticated technological tools and materials to dive in this field, and how much communities of practice are contributing in generating knowledge and methodology from experts.

The theoretical framework will be focused on the different practice fields: *cognitive apprenticeship*, *metacognition*, and *situated learning* that we will explain through the design of Udemy community of practice.

This part of the chapter is combining two things that we are trying to work on: novice instructional designer combined with novice learner inside a community of practice. Both characteristics are connected with the fact that a novice instructional designer will always need to merge into professional practitioners to be able to reshape their skills, as these communities can give an amount of learning that any other school cannot.

Communities of practice provide solutions, information, tools, resources, and much more until you become comfortable in your field. They put your learning into evidence and merge your skills into the market where you can measure your ability now and what you need to work on for later.

In this community, novice instructors join to collect the necessary information that will help them deliver high-quality eLearning and engage adult learners. It is a challenge for every novice instructor to self-direct themselves and learn the usage of the material in balancing technology with teaching skills. Therefore, we will highlight the principles of adult learning and include a process on how to develop andragogical teaching skills.

Our generation is going through different experiences where adults must change habits to learn and to cope with the new challenges in adult learning. This shift in learning is a move from an *instructional* to *constructional learning approach*. The learner has more responsibilities in constructivist environment where he can choose his learning process and create situations to build his knowledge.

In constructivist theory, this process is about how to achieve learning (Black and McClintock, 1995) rather than what to learn. In communities of practice, adult learners can learn without having the feeling that they are learning. *"Engagement in social practice is the fundamental process by which we get to know what we know and by which we become who we are"* (Wenger, 1998).

This learning environment is important to demonstrate one's experiences and practices in a certain community. To explain this point of view, we refer to Dewey (1916, 74) who wrote that the *"experience itself primarily consists of the active relations subsisting between a human being and his natural and social surroundings.*" Thus, within a community, we can interact and reflect on our knowledge with others through the action of learning.

To explore more on the process of learning in constructivist environment, we will discuss how an instructor can build his profile, platform, and courses with Udemy. It is an application where you can sell and buy courses online. Udemy created a community to teach novice instructors several strategies and tips to be able to build quality learning. You can enroll to this community and explore the criteria and strategies used to engage the adult learners and how to restructure the learning process in eLearning environment, and to understand how theories are employed in CoP using Udemy's community of practice.

a. Cognitive Apprenticeship

Online learning is expanding to become a powerful tool for both educators and learners. It is now easier than before to find and enroll to any course of our choice according to our interests. All we need is a server and motivation to accomplish our learning in an informal community. Wertsch (2012, 109) wrote, "*Virtually all human action, be it on the individual or social interactional plane, is socioculturally situated.*" Harasim (2012) notes that learning in communities of practice is experimental; we learn by observing, by doing, and by experiencing.

The transformation of knowledge from experiences to an artifact or a product is called *reification* (Harasim, 2012). That is what we learn to do in Udemy's community. It is an important stage for any novice instructor to gather his knowledge and experiences of a classroom teacher and transform them into an artifact, which is a complete course posted online.

b. From Novice to Expert

Novice instructors will need to interact with experts to learn about this field. *Cognitive apprenticeship approach* defines this stage

17

where knowledge is transformed from expert to novice member. In Collins' article (1991), there is a beautiful expression about cognitive apprenticeship where it is defined as *"Making Thinking Visible."* It is exactly what we're going to see: the process starting from the final product and breaking it down to understand the several stages of how to conduct and deliver a quality course.

However, novice learners will face real-world problems and will need to have support from experienced members while conducting activities that relates to the problem-solving. Novice learners will face a lot of barriers while trying to solve the problem they faced. Their engagement might decrease, and they might leave the community.

To guarantee their continuity, the community must interact with these new instructors through activities and workshops by providing tips and showing the right tools to build an effective e-course. Barb (1998) writes that *"these activities must be authentic. They must present most of the cognitive demands the learner would encounter in the 'real world'."*

This continuous help and scaffold provided to the new members will form the historical element of the community. Experienced instructors are an important element in providing continuity to the community. As we all know, new members need to be engaged to keep using the community: If they lose interest, they can quit in the first week of joining the community.

However, the experienced instructors who are present in the community can share crucial knowledge and contribute in maintaining a historical heritage to the community. Creating a common heritage of the community *"through telling and retelling"* (Barb 1998) can be more than passing out the knowledge to the novice instructors; it creates consistency and history for their community.

c. Engagement and Motivation

Engagement and motivation are the glue that keeps the community growing while developing trust between the members and creating proactive meetings, constructive dialogues, and debates in a well-structured platform.

The domain, the community, and the practice are three elements that build a trustful platform, and balancing between these elements is a key factor for a CoP to succeed. The sharing of knowledge is usually motivated by the common language, interests, and visions (Chiu and Wang, 2006), which influence members to share their expertise with confidence.

d. Peer Feedback

This is also an important element to guide new members to the right behavior or teach them the right way in accomplishing their activities within the standards of the community. Peer feedback can improve learning and individuals' performance. It is a *metacognitive approach* (Lu and Law, 2012) that is effective for all members, including peripheral novice members.

Peer feedback helps to conduct a reflection on self-engagement and to identify problems in certain situations and to find solutions for common problems.

e. Collaboration

Collaboration is one of the most important elements that has to be developed in a community of practice. Collaborative work can enhance the fluidity of work (Faraj et al., 2011), it provides the learner with a dynamic learning experience, and it generates resources and builds knowledge.

Now let's see all these factors inside a working community to understand how to put these theories and approaches into practice.

6. Udemy, Theory in Practice

Under this section, we're going to put the above learning theories of communities of practice into action. We will explain how these approaches become useful for the learner when they are all gathered in one place to build skills and competencies in many ways: technical and practical skills.

a. From Novice to Expert

Udemy is an online community of practice that provides the educators with an approach for learning from each other and from experts, how to build an online course, and how to market it.

Udemy's management has requirements to achieve at the instructors' side: they want you to deliver a quality course to their learners (clients) to be able to compete in the market with other e-course providers. It is a well-structured community that is controlled by several rules and invites all the instructors to respect a specific schedule.

The major benefit an instructor can have from Udemy's community is the training that the management of the community provides to the new instructors. Once you joined the community with an instructor profile, your dashboard will receive automatic videos (courses) from where you can learn how to make high-quality e-courses and how to attract a big number of students, and these are the guiding tools and services that we can get automatically as novice instructors to comply with the standards of the platform and, hence, the market requirements.

The community's role is clear: marketing the courses of the instructors and get paid accordingly (50 percent of the course price). The e-course is set at sixty minutes that the instructor dispatches into several videos and resources. Udemy, as its marketing strategy, looks up for quality courses that the instructor can sell for more than $100. This strategy is excellent for people who don't want to get into the hassle of marketing and stick to the intellectual role of the instructor.

b. Engagement and Motivation

New instructors need daily basic technical support. In Udemy's community, novices ask frequent questions about the best microphone to use, the kind of writing tablets they need, how to measure the light in the room, or how to reduce noises from a speech track. Experts reply to these questions each from their perspective, the tools available in their region, the prices, and the brands available in the market. All these tips given by experts in the field are valuable information that anyone can spend a lot of time searching on the internet to get some of the details that might not be good in practice.

In this platform, experienced instructors are providing useful answers from their own learning experience and valuable information that makes the community a place where people learn constantly and develop good practices. The community itself is becoming a source of knowledge and works constantly to provide artifacts that help the learners build their skills according to the standards of the community. It is a structured informal community that has rules and boundaries to respect, and that is what makes every challenge the novice instructor faces coherent.

Novice instructors can fail in attracting students to their videos. So their quality videos can fail in sales and their well-resourced course can fail in attracting new learners as well. Experienced instructors can provide tips and tricks to raise the sales factor and improve the cost of the videos. They can explain why a course is not getting many likes or why learners are dropping the course before they go further in it. We are not talking about experienced instructors only, but we have another bonus element to look after, In fact they are online professional and experienced instructors who have good sales too.

To sell your video fast, it means that you could engage your learners, attract new learners, and provide the same content that other instructors are selling in a new way or in a different perspective that could cover different types of learners. To do so, you will need more than a quality course; you will need to go through the other courses that provide the same content and check them all to find out where you are going to focus on your course or how to make them choose your e-course. Usually, online learners choose the newest information given. They like when the lesson is deconstructed then reconstructed; they prefer chunked e-course on steps and self-assessments or quizzes at the end of each step to feel that they manipulate the content, and they also like to be engaged with situated activities. At the end, you will find yourself organizing your e-course in a way that the technical quality will no longer matter for your learner as long as the learning outcome (profit) is high.

To keep novice instructors interested in the community, even after they failed in marketing their e-course, the community opens a communication channel to provide them with a logical explanation about *why* they failed. Once they could understand the why, they will try again, taking into consideration all the comments and explanations given by the experts. They feel that they need to try again especially when they notice that the problem they are facing did happen before with someone else, another novice instructor who feels now confident and is selling fast his e-courses.

Remember that we're mentioning the marketing side of the e-courses because this is our measurement for an effective e-course in Udemy.

Experts can make available their knowledge because they were once in the same situation and could get support from other experts; that is why they are now motivated to communicate their knowledge as they all share the same interest. Self-efficacy and outcome expectations are major factors in guiding people to share their knowledge. If the members believe that they can achieve an activity, then they will be motivated by their inner belief of success.

For adult learning, the criteria and strategies used for online learning to engage the learners are much more related to the objectives of the individuals within the community, and the focus is precisely on solving the learning issues, and giving support to the novice instructors while merging in the field. It is also required to assist them through resources and provide clear tasks through practice or learning situations. Attracting new people to the community to merge new ideas and conduct discussions to make these new ideas understandable for all members is what keeps the community evolving constantly.

To restructure the learning process in eLearning constructivist environment, it is crucial to do the following:

- o Create authentic content allowing the learner to be opened on the newest information
- o Install strategies for self-paced learning and practices
- o Give control and assign responsibilities to the learners on their community by involving them in taking turns on the different tasks of the community members

Finally, the community itself is a useful and healthy place for adult learners (instructors and students) to open up on the different skills and get updated information about any topic of interest that the community might discuss. The resources and the tips and tricks are always an added value for all community members.

c. Peer Feedback

Feedback from peers is a collaborative and constructivist learning strategy that ensures a good outcome in learning. Peer feedback can help Udemy's instructors to work collaboratively on a course. It gives novice instructors instant feedback from experts who reflect on their work, which will promote critical thinking inside the community. As Wiggens explains (1993), to acquire good habits-of-mind, learners should comment on one another's learning outcomes to conduct effective learning and get meaningful knowledge.

Over time, the novice instructors will show improvement in self-regulated learning, increase their motivation, and learn how to focus on their educational goals and outcomes. This strategic metacognition contributes in making the learner self-directed and goes through four stages: establish the learning goals; plan for the learning; monitor the learning (try it); and reflect on the learning then come back again to the first point and establish new goals to measure learning.

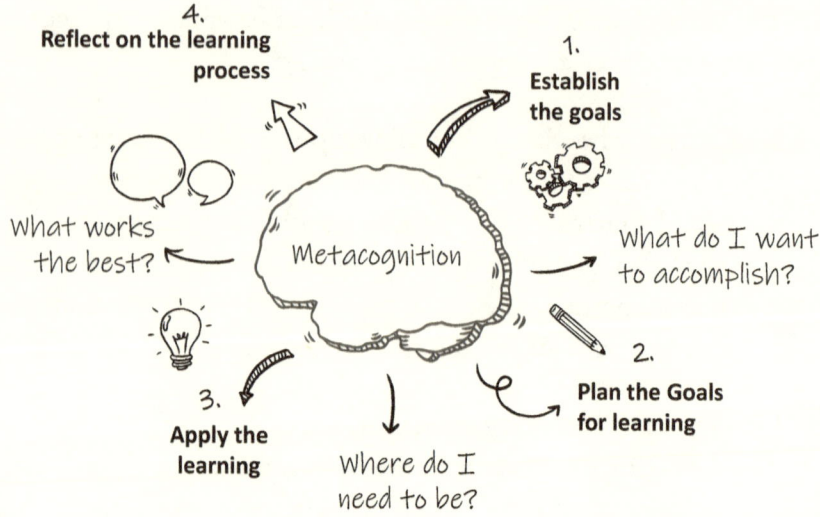

Figure 1. Metacognition for self-directed learning.

d. Collaboration

During the peripheral participation in Udemy's community, the novice instructor might notice that there are e-courses that are constructed collaboratively between two or more instructors and that this interaction with each other aims to make their learning effective within the community by building a collaborative e-course where novices interact with mature practitioners to conduct a professional e-course in a certain field. This is recognized as *social nature of learning*, where novice learners cannot solve a problem by their own and call for help from professionals in the field to get the right cognitive scaffolding and challenge themselves outside their comfort zone. Before they move from their comfort zone to the challenge they face, they go through a social process that Vygotsky considers as a social process to reach a cognitive development (zone of proximal development or, for short, ZPD).

This apprenticeship journey is an effective way to train novice instructors and integrate them in the CoP. Some prefer to interact with novices like them to feel comfortable in joining the experience at their pace. The important element in novice-to-novice interaction is the role of the community in scaffolding their experience by sending them constant e-mails to teach them how to conduct a quality e-course via artifacts that a novice instructor receives from the community, like interactive PDFs to plan their e-courses, videos (tutorials), tips and tricks, and instructional strategies embedded in theories. They also send notifications at each stage while the novice instructor tries to build up his e-course and propose solutions for the problems the instructor might face at each stage.

Now, let's work on the same idea of CoPs in schools. What if we decided to incorporate andragogical theories and practices in a pedagogical environment?

AFTER-SCHOOL COMMUNITIES OF PRACTICE

Let's try an application of what we learned in this chapter by combining pedagogy and andragogy with the concept of communities of practice (Aguilar and Krasny, 2011). If we decided to design an after-school program to teach to the primary students what the CoPs are and how to be an effective member in such communities as this will help them later in their virtual communities, the primary step is to shape their skills in this matter and give them the right to act as adult learners by choosing their learning. To apply the idea of CoPs in after-school clubs, we're going to create several clubs. Each club is self-emergent: the students will discuss to find topics to their clubs, then they will try to convince other students to join it. The students will have to find the right resources they need to produce artifacts and to decorate their club to attract other members. These artifacts must be a collective work. Only clubs with a big number of students will "survive" until the end of the month.

We will ask the students to collaborate on every product and provide scaffolding to the students who do not have the right skills to accomplish the tasks set at the beginning by the club members.

At the end of the month, the school will decide on the emergent club, the most popular and the best in producing artifacts with the most engaged members.

The framework we can use to apply on such clubs is called a *sociocultural situated cognition*, using joint enterprise, mutual engagement, and shared repertoire. Situated cognition theory states that human actions are adapted from their environments and that what people learn, see, and do is situated in their role as a member of community (Lave and Wenger, 1991).

DESIGN FOR VISUALITY

For an effective learning outcome, embracing high visuality is a good practice to follow when we design for online learners. This strategy can make a big amount of information well organized and better understood in a short time. Infographics, mind maps, and advance organizers are the best learning aids any instructional designer can use to enhance the visuality of the e-course.

ADVANCE ORGANIZERS AND COGNITIVE LOAD THEORY

Advance organizers are a concept that came from Ausubel's cognitive science theory. This psychologist assumes that *"people acquire knowledge primarily by being exposed directly to it rather than through discovery"* (Woolfolk et al., 2010, 288).

Advance organizers can provide information directly to the student to enhance retention and self-reflection. It is a cognitive concept that instructional designers can include at the beginning of instruction or as a part of the recapitulation of concepts and facts.

In eLearning, students can feel overwhelmed with all the resources and new knowledge they can have for one topic and the amount of information to process. This is due to the *cognitive load* they faced that can be intrinsic (complexity of the new information) or extraneous (exterior distractions); both cognitive loads must be changed into a germane load (connect the new information to prior knowledge or schema) to enhance retention and processing of the new topic.

To avoid such load in learning, the designer can arrange the learning platform in a way that makes the complexity of the information easy to process by chunking the new topic into small learning bites with specific learning outcomes.

On the other hand, students can be asked to use advance organizers to reduce their confusion at the beginning of the session and produce their own organizers to show their understanding of the different aspects of the topic or reflect by connecting the information they learned at the end of the session. Let's take a closer look at some of these advance organizers and their roles.

1. Concept Map

The concept map is the result of Ausubel's thinking on meaningful learning. It helps visualize different points of the lesson in one location, and learners can edit or read it. Many empirical studies were conducted to measure the importance of concept maps in learning (learning through visual displays). In some studies, concept maps were found useful and the understanding of learners is found higher when constructing visualized organizers. In some other studies, they are found helpful but not as efficient as writing text summaries or word-based reflections.

However, concept maps are highly recommended in eLearning where students can visualize the relationship between the different structures and the objectives of the topic in an effective manner referred to as design thinking. The concept map is clear, direct, and easy to understand, and is a creative way to plan, explain, and organize ideas, and reflect on the lesson. They can be used as an exit ticket in eLearning sessions too. If used at the beginning of the session, it gives an overview of the knowledge the student is going to expand and explains how the lesson is built up (germane cognitive load).

It also helps determine the prior knowledge of the students at the introduction of the topic and find the gap in learning to introduce new knowledge elements when prior knowledge is absent (extraneous cognitive load).

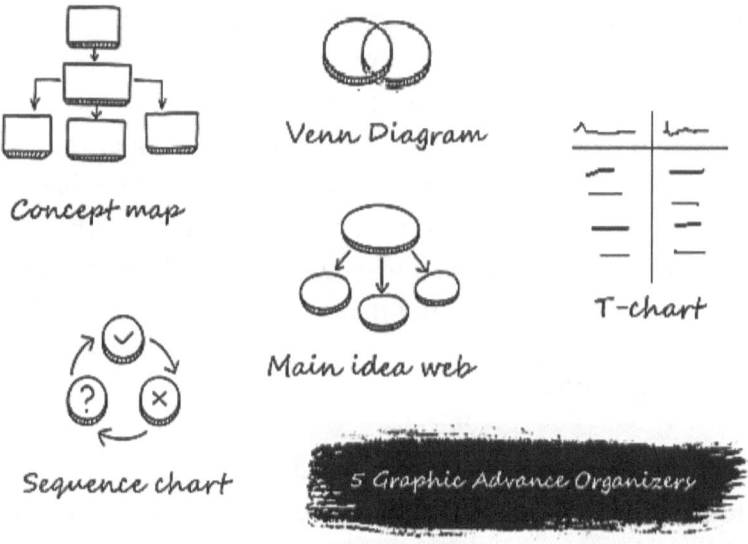

Figure 2. Five graphic advance organizers. Available at https://mcdreeamiemusings.com/blog/2019/10/15/the-good-the-bad-and-the-can-be-ugly-the-three-parts-of-cognitive-load

2. Sequence Chart

The sequence chart is another type of graphic organizer that can be used to enhance retention, and precisely, to show the different parts and sequences of the topic and be able to organize them into numbers or steps. Students can use a sequence chart to plan their learning and to scaffold an idea or a topic. They can demonstrate the different parts of the story in a reading and comprehension course; they can break a scientific topic into steps to have a deeper understanding or simplify a detailed topic. They can use it to apply more detailed descriptions to the steps, explain ideas on a specific project of their own, or contribute to building a collaborative step-by-step project.

3. Venn Diagram

This organizer is an effective tool to create relationships between two things and to understand two topics by comparing their features and facets and by putting all the elements together in a clear way. It can be used by teachers and students in eLearning to summarize two or more ideas and relate them to each other by highlighting the similarities and differences. It is a logic mapping that can help wrap-up several topics in one visual aid.

At the end, it is to mention that most learning is conducted via smart platforms that are built by specialists, psychologists, and instructional designers to provide a suitable learning experience for the students. The role of the instructor is usually to motivate, guide, and assess the learner according to what he needs, and to involve, engage, and promote community building and interesting discussions among the students.

The direct input of the instructor tends to vanish when students can get the resources in an organized way on a given online platform; as these automated platforms are getting smarter, they can cover most of the traditional mechanic roles of the instructor, like correcting the assignments, distributing tasks, informing the learners about important dates, and sending notifications to the parents and the students.

When online learning emerged, the early version of these platforms was designing a learner-centered website to cover the e-course requirements and to conduct collaborative learning as these websites were shared with the students for editing and submission of their work.

As an example to what a designer can compile for the delivery of an individual e-course, we prepared a sample platform that is student-centered and task-based learning with the flexibility of mobile learning (mLearning). This e-course is made to serve a certain situation where the designer had to engineer with the aid of multiple theories to be able to construct a new version of a student-centered e-course.

E-Course Design

The scope of this project is to design and deliver an effective e-course for a self-learning experience that a private school is trying to start for the benefit of their students. The school decided that the French subject is not easy any more with the implementation of online learning, and it is time to make it a self-learning subject.

Students will log in to the platform (a website-based e-course) and learn alone with no teacher and with self-assessment at the end of each module. The school is informing the students that they are self-taught, but the results of their learning will be added in their grade book and final reports.

The course to be designed is a French course that a private school needs for their primary students. It will be delivered online, and it is called Français Au Quotidien, and it is a website-based course.

Course Description

The school decided that the French course is not easy any more with the implementation of online learning, and it is time to make it a self-learning subject. Students will log in to the platform and learn alone with no teacher. Then, they will have to make a self-assessment at the end of each module. The school is informing the students that they are self-taught, but the results of their learning will be added to their grade book and final reports.

1. Problem to Solve

This project came as a solution to a challenging situation brought to the light with the COVID-19 arrangements for online learning. Students showed no interest in learning French, and most of them were not showing up in the synchronous classes nor accomplishing their tasks assigned by their French teacher.

2. Description

The school needed to allocate an *online course in the French language* to teach students from grade 3 to 9 with no instructor: a self-learning course, mobile delivered, and task-based with very specific objectives and modules, where their students can learn alone.

The school decided that the e-course is not an elective subject; it is a required course, and the results of the students will show in their grade book and final reporting system.

3. Main Goals and Objectives

The school informed the designers that this e-course should be extended to wider objectives than to teach French to their students. The following steps demonstrate the learning goals, objectives, and outcomes adapted from Tom Angelo's workshop (2013):

> GOAL: Students from grade 3 to grade 9 will be effective self-directed learners, highly motivated, and responsible for their learning while building new skills in speaking and writing the French language.

> WHAT: Students will be able to locate tasks, self-learn, and self-assess while learning to write and speak the French language.

HOW WELL (expectations): Students will become self-directed learners with speaking and writing skills in the French language (beginner levels 1, 2, and 3).

HOW (course format): Online course designed specifically for the school curriculum.

WHEN: At the end of the school year.

4. The Audience

The audience of this project includes all enrolled students in the school from grade 3 to grade 9 who are learning French as a third language and are beginners according to the language level set by the curriculum of the school (level 1, 2, and 3 beginners). They are students from different backgrounds and languages.

5. Prerequisites

To take this course, students should be enrolled in the school, knowing the basics of using an external platform and the capability to navigate through the website to be able to find the course and work independently. The e-course is offering a tutorial at the beginning to show to the students how to initiate the instruction and conduct effective learning sessions.

The language course is for level 0 to level 3 advanced students. No prerequisites in knowing the language are required for level 0, while the prerequisites for level 1, 2, and 3 are linked to the previous level acquired.

COURSE DESIGN

1. Time, Logistics, and Sequences

The time frame of this course is a long-term e-course, as the school will allow it for the rest of the year. The number of students who will enroll in this course are four hundred from different backgrounds, cultures, and languages.

The school has French textbooks for all grade levels included in the program but decided that selected content can be integrated into the e-course from the textbooks with alteration of the delivery mode of the content.

2. Course Approaches

Many theories of learning and approaches were deployed to construct the foundational elements of the design of this e-course. First of all, we decided that a *Connectivist Theory* (Siemens, 2005) will enhance the design and empower the main objectives of the school in creating a collaborative environment, increasing self-learning capabilities in primary and middle school with twenty-first-century skills.

The learning process is developed with the guidance of the instructor through the tools and the material used (mentioned under the title Collaboration and Interaction) and relies on learner-centered approaches that the personal devices can boost. That is why our e-course has a friendly design that allows the users to study from their phones directly and accomplish the tasks required weekly with no problem in visuality or interactivity of the material.

Drill and practice is also an approach that connectivism allows with the integration of multimedia tools where students can try and retry, and no negative feedback will be given to them. They have all the material displayed for them to locate the information needed and the web to consult more resources. They can post their work, come back again, and post it for a second time and more with no limited submission date. This strategy can allow them to improve their work whenever they feel uncomfortable with the first submission.

We integrated interaction and collaboration based on Jonassen's model (1999) of constructivist learning environments (CLEs), who explains how technology can facilitate collaboration and construction of knowledge with social interaction. CLEs engage students in investigating the information, criticizing the problem, and reviewing the resources.

The framework we followed to design the e-course is based on 7Cs framework (Conole, 2013) for designing eLearning that is made to guide teachers in designing practices and activities that engage using technology as the key concept in designing explicit experience through visual representations, sharable knowledge, and interactive community of learners.

The 7Cs framework is an added value to the course design:

- Conceptualize the content by personalizing it to the learners' needs using different approaches.
- Capture open educational resources and develop new resources
- Create learning interventions and activities to engage the learner.
- Communicate using multiple ways to avoid isolation of the learner.
- Collaboration is important to scaffold learning and create a community.
- Consider new types of reflection and demonstration of learning, new activities, and assessment strategies.
- Consolidate the effectiveness of the e-course design and its workability with different devices and in different situations.

To be able to apply the 7Cs framework, the designers created a website for the course as a platform for course delivery and submission of the students' work. It allowed the designers to adjust the content, the display, and the tasks according to the framework chosen for a flexible learning experience.

We also created tailored content for the learners to make the course diversified and organized with different tools as explained in the next title.

Universal instructional design for online learning is a framework that we used to support our learning environment and be able to cover the maximum of learners' abilities and disabilities:

-   The flexibility of the design being used in the e-course can help the student interact easily with the content using several personal devices. The content is well chunked and presented in bits of information to avoid confusion as it requires a self-learning process.
-   The design of the e-course was carefully made to be consistent, which reflects on the repeated type of tasks that the course offers each week to avoid any new strategies of work that might interrupt the learning process and give the chance to several disabilities to adapt to the course design.
-   For better accessibility to the materials chosen for the e-course, we applied many formats to the material and resources: audio, video, PPTs, PDFs, etc. This is to allow students with different capabilities to interact with the content the way they choose to. As the e-course is a new language for the students, the different tasks rely on providing audios for the students along with a written version of the text and translations when needed to be able to accomplish the task with the scaffolding from the audios and videos.
-   In an attempt to minimize the efforts, students can work directly on the platform and submit their work from any device even from their mobiles. This flexibility came to help students who do not know how to install French keyboards in their computers to be able to write French characters from their mobile phones.
-   The environment of this e-course supports the learners as it gives them a space to answer directly. No hassle needed to submit their work, they can answer directly on the designated space and submit their work. An external cloud is used from

Google Drive as a cloud computing system that students can access and are already well informed about its affordances and facilitations.

3. Collaboration and Interaction

Under this title, we will discuss how we opened opportunities for the students to interact with the content of the course, with other learners, and with the instructor using several tools and technologies while following the 7Cs framework (Conole, 2013):

— For the *conceptualization of the content*, we used the same pattern of the lesson all over the grade-level material to allow the student to interact with the content with hyperlinks, videos, audios, and buttons for downloads and uploads; but we insisted on maintaining a pattern of interaction. Changing the organization and the look of the lesson for online learners can create confusion and give them a feeling of being unable to follow the lesson or understand the required tasks especially for primary school students.

— Using *open resources* is something that helped us design a free course. One of the tools we used is the Memoji that everyone has in his iPhone to create videos and simulations for a teacher and give instructions or dictations (learner-to-teacher interaction). Memojis can simulate the movement of the lips, which is helpful for dictations. Other open French resources were used for reading and writing practices like *developing new resources* from PPT and convert them into videos with the teachers' voices to enhance understanding and guide the learners in the French pronunciation as a scaffold for learning.

— We used a *task-based structure* to build the lessons (diversified tasks throughout the week). This strategy allowed us to *communicate in different ways* our content to the learner (learner-to-content interaction). Each week, students will have daily tasks to accomplish. New tasks were triggered by the accomplishment of the old task (technology existing in website design and mLearning). This strategy can help students accomplish their learning in the right order and guide them throughout the lesson.

– To *avoid isolation of the learners*, we implemented in this course a forum that allows the students and the instructor to upload and download audio files, videos, and Memojis with teacher's recording, and more diverted entries to cover the topic where students can answer the teacher's questions (learner-to-teacher interaction) and be able to share their responses on social media (web usage) or WhatsApp and showcase their learning (learner-to-community interaction) by reflecting and demonstrating their gained skills. Forums can contribute in providing scaffolding to slower learners from knowledgeable learners and instructors who interact with the content by posting artifacts as a response to a task or a question.

– We also added to the course a chat room where students can choose members to create groups of learners (learner-to-learner interaction), open a new entry by asking questions or talking about a problem they are facing while learning (scaffolding again). Even parents can participate in the chat rooms, as they are designed to accept e-mails from outside the community of learners. This way, students will build a feeling of belonging to a community that they know is from the school to enhance engagement and motivation for the course and reduce dropping-off incidences.

4. Assessments

The e-course relies on many assessment strategies that aim to keep the student informed. It is important for the school to control the performance of the students and to review the material whenever it fails to serve the goals and objectives of the curriculum and the course. Learning modules are the learning units, including assessments, students will take during this course, which is based on thirty-two weeks of online learning (one school year). Each unit will take five weeks of different topics, including four quizzes (one quiz per week) and one assessment (at the fifth week).

"Test Your Knowledge" quizzes are the type of quizzes we decided will help our students reviewing the content they were working on the whole week. It is a way to guide them in case they did not notice any detail that is considered important and to give them a better understanding of the objectives set for the week. Instant feedback with indications to the right answer is used in the quizzes, along with the possibility to redo the quiz at the convenience of the student.

Dictations (few words or sentences) and speaking practices using audio/video files are also included in the weekly tasks to test the students' abilities to write the new language. Listening comprehension practices (longer texts) are included as well to maintain all the skills aligned with the objectives of the course.

At the end of the unit, the students will undergo a final assessment for all the topics taken during this time to sum up their efforts and collect their grades for the school. During this week, no new topic will be added to the e-course; they will be seeing only practices/quizzes to prepare them for the final assessment. The assessment will be conducted on the platform (website) and will have instant feedback to motivate and guide them throughout the test. Students with low scores will have to take a makeup test two days later.

5. Learner Support

To support the learner, the e-course design provides a helpdesk team to support the learner whenever they needed to. They can ask questions, call, send an sms, e-mail from the Contact Us button, or send a voice message to the team for any help.

A chat box is added to the course structure for instant feedback where the students can type in directly their questions to the helpdesk or the instructors whenever they need assistance.

The chat box will send messages to the application of the teacher or the helpdesk on the other side of the chat as a notification message. This consolidates the structure of the course that is offering self-learning to support the learners whenever they feel unable to accomplish a task or submit their work. The school has assigned academics to follow up with the students for technical support and learning achievements

Designing a course to be delivered fully online is a hard task to entertain. It requires attention to the smallest details and engineering approaches that work altogether to end up with a balanced structure and e-course. We faced so many constraints just because of the age of our audience, which urged us to make the course design attractive, flexible, easy to access from mobile, and easy to accomplish with lesser distractions.

Another constraint we faced is the requirement to design a self-learning course that is incorporated in the school report, which made the design a responsibility that was driving our work to make it valuable and valid for the school and useful for the students.

Mobile learning affordances allowed us to enrich our resources and deploy our knowledge for the technology to create cost-free content without worrying about copyrights.

Chapter II
ELEARNING DESIGN

In this chapter, we are going to look closely at the different delivery forms of eLearning to decorticate the different aspects, models, and frames that make a platform a smart, innovative, and effective educational tool for a large community of students. It is important though to incorporate innovative technics in smart learning environments to enrich the student experience.

A learning model is a combination of the process you, as an instructional designer, want your students to learn. To combine this process and shape it in the best way to suit your learning objectives, goals, and environment, there is only one way to do that: review your learning theories (Uljens, 2004). There are many effective instructional design models that any novice designer can use to build effective strategies using theories of learning: the ADDIE model, Gagné's nine events of instruction model, the Kemp instructional design model, the ASSURE model, Merrill's principles of instruction model, and the SAM model.

As we're working on eLearning instruction, Merrill's model is the best to suit your designs, as it is made for learning that is delivered online through VLEs. It is also good to show the stages of this model to your teachers and how they can use it to build constructive learning in their presentations, as it is a student-centered model of work that suits most of the subjects taught at elementary and middle school.

First, let's review the model and its learning steps and strategies.

MERRILL'S MODEL OF INSTRUCTION (2002)

For student-centered learning design, Merrill's model of instruction suits most of the learners in online platforms. It is made to design VLEs; that is why it is task-centered learning based on five principles.

LEARNER-CENTERED	Learning is promoted when learners...
PROBLEM-BASED	Acquire knowledge and skills in the context of real-world problems and tasks.
ACTIVATION	Recall or apply existing knowledge and skills as a foundation for new skills.
DEMONSTRATION	Observe and guide a demonstration of the knowledge and skills to be learned
APPLICATION	Use their newly acquired knowledge and skills to solve new problems or carry out new tasks from the real world.
INTEGRATION	Discuss, defend and reflect on the newly acquired skill by integrating the skill into a real-world activity.

Adapted from Merrill's Principles of Instruction (Merrill, 2012).

Figure 3. Merrill's principles of instruction (2012).

Task-centered learning in eLearning platforms is similar to the hands-on activities in a classroom setting, where the learner is required to accomplish a task after task to cover the course topics.

The tasks are based on four steps: Activation of the learning, demonstration, application, and integration. To complete these tasks, the student is required first to activate his previous learning, demonstrate his understanding, then apply what was learned throughout the tasks required to accomplish. At the end, the learner will need to integrate what was learned by including it in his experience or work.

Even though it is important to highlight that, before choosing the right ID for your instruction, the planning of the instructional design should include specific learning objectives such as the cognitive strategies, the information to deliver verbally, and the intellectual skills required to reach the required learning goals to be able to choose the right instructional design for the course in question (Gagné and Merrill, 1990).

Integrating Innovative, Creative, and Smart Learning

However, what makes an instruction innovative, creative, and smart? How to effectively implement these factors? How to measure the creativity that an instructional design can provide to its learners, and how to identify the major elements needed to build innovative and smart learning strategies?

To answer these questions, we will go through a case study from the literature. A project that aims to enhance the learning experience for FLE students in higher education in Indonesia.

1. Flipped-Classroom Approach

To start an instructional design from scratch, it is important to know your audience, to define your goals and objectives, and then to allocate your tools and resources to meet your goals. The approaches for learning are numerous, and to effectively define the approaches you need for your project, it is important to plan for your instruction and know your objectives, your learners, and the format needed for delivery. Planning is very important as a key stage for an effective and successful eLearning design. Some approaches and learning theories can be matched perfectly to complement the instruction, guide the designer in choosing the tools and the strategies for learning, and find the right framework (steps of work) that the literature proposes. Sometimes, you need to alternate the design to suit the learning outcome and objectives; in some others, you need to fix the gaps found in the objectives to cover the learning framework, which represents the guidelines to achieve a balanced instructional design.

The instructional design we are going to decorticate in this chapter aims to help some junior instructors understand what the approach they need the most when they start building their ID is. This research paper can be considered a roadmap to junior instructors, especially with the COVID-19 pandemic that boosted eLearning, and most of the instructions are transferred to online platforms. It is necessary though to understand the approach that will suit UAE learners and how to apply it in a school environment.

The paper we are going to focus on (Zainuddin, 2018) is a design-centered research approach (DBR) for instructional technology. The research aims to create a new design to shift learning from textbook-centered to student-centered and to encourage self-direction and higher thinking skills; and these are considered the primary goals of this ID. We chose this paper because it is a close approach to what is going on here in UAE schools and how the instruction is shifted from traditional to flipped-classroom approach.

It is also an occasion to show how to use Bloom's taxonomy, which is very common in UAE schools, and how to use it in an instruction that is delivered online.

The research is made through a work process: planning, designing, formative evaluation, revising, redesigning, and summative evaluation. The instructional design is following the revised Bloom's taxonomy (cognitive framework) where the instructional designer chose to use a bottom-up taxonomy to be able to flip the learning and present it to the learner in another perspective:

- Remembering and understanding stages are covered outside the classroom.
- Applying, analyzing, evaluating, and creating are applied inside the classroom.

The higher thinking skills are gained with peers and in the classroom to encourage the students to be more productive and less passive during the course delivery.

The flipped classroom is considered blended learning that provides to the students all necessary course materials on a technological platform, which is a learning management system (in this project: Schoology), where the instructors can upload the material to be studied before the physical course. The LMS platform is friendly and easy to use by the students. The learning outcomes of this instructional design are measured through the motivation and the collaboration between the students during the class sessions where learning is conducted through discussions, storytelling, debates, and group work; while the assessments are given on the platform through quizzes, case studies, and group projects.

In this ID, the designer used many resources uploaded to the learning platform, which were mainly videos, from different providers like National Geographic, BBC News, and TED-ex. The choice came from the fact that the literature review recommends the usage of different resources using different software.

To measure how much smart learning and innovative techniques are used by the instructional designer of this project, we will have to explain first the following: What is smart learning? What makes a design innovative? And how can one be creative while building an ID and integrate creativity element to the student's platform?

Smart Learning

Smart learning does not mean precisely to use smart technologies for the delivery of the course. It has to be effective and engaging for the students. That is why to evaluate the smart learning of this ID, we need first to understand how much the flipped classroom helped the students receive effective learning and how much the platform is friendly and comprehensive for the learners (Wang and Heffernan, 2009). According to the designer of this study, implementing a flipped-classroom model is not as easy as recording videos and preparing material for a wide variety of students. The content must be attractive and fun to watch; it must engage the students to open the platform and work by themselves using gaming and reinforcements, providing badges, and giving instant feedback through the messaging system that the platform provides to the instructors.

The adjective *smart* indicates that the process is going through careful planning, personalized and meaningful learning with instant and personalized feedback. However, we will be exploring the framework of what we call a smart learning environment, and the following are some of its important characteristics:

1. Necessary (Effective and Scalable)

It is to build a learning design that has effective learning outcomes and where the learning is considered engaging. To incorporate valuable futuristic ideas to prepare the learner for now and for later, it has to be effective for all the audience, to implement a structured context and methodologies that open the learners' minds on how to activate their skills instead of passively "learn to forget." If the learning environment is quite effective, it will be easy to fit in a larger audience like national and international learners.

Scalable learning is implemented by diversifying the content to suit a larger number of learners and employ several technological tools and resources to facilitate the perception of the content and facilitate the sharing of skills and knowledge. Scalable learning is a student-driven approach that John Hagel mentioned for the first time for business development content (Hagel et al., 2009). He recognized scalable learning focuses on learning through actions, a peer-to-peer learning, and in-the-workflow learning. It is to put them into action and let them be challenged to learn what they need to know instead of telling them what they are supposed to learn. It is to ignite the passion of the explorer to keep the learners stimulated and to help them become innovative.

According to John Hagel, scalable learning is to create new situations and problems that the learner has never seen before and let them dig into the problem and develop skills in small groups to solve the problems. It required collaboration to create effective scalable learning.

Consequently, the design will be based on the creation of a smart learning environment to enhance collective learning and collaboration. In this case study, the instructional designer took into consideration the fact that in the Indonesian university, there are different ideologies, languages, and cultures that should be working collectively during the class sessions. In this way, the idea of creating a flipped classroom could help the instructor provide quality collaborative sessions to the students of FLE, where debates, discussions, and group work are the main activities for the physical classes.

Integrating collaboration in this instruction is going to break the wall of differentiation and construct bonds between the learners, which will improve the sense of the learning community on top of the effectivity of the learning itself.

2. Highly Desirable

Being highly desirable is to create motivation that lasts and sustainable learning that is considered interesting for many types of learners. To be able to do that, learning design has to be flexible (adjustable at any time) to cover the needs of new learners who will join the course later; it has to present diversified material that suits a variety of learners and to adjust the learning outcomes to the learners' skills and abilities. Once done, the designer has to personalize the learning design by a variety of assessments or personalized feedback that can help struggling students and support fast learners as well.

In this research, the instructional designer could cover this section through the usage of a platform that is engaging and has a friendly design, as it is easy for any teacher to organize his content and display his tasks and assignments in a clear and structured way. In addition to that, it is easy to merge the new-coming learners as they can go through the uploaded courses and study on their pace until they feel ready to join the course. The LMS used can be easily personalized to the students, as each student can see the content that is meant for him; the assignments and quizzes can be linked to the learning outcomes or benchmarks of the state.

3. Conversational, Reflective, and Innovative

An engaging environment for learning can be realized through different strategies by creating conversational situations (forums, debates, group discussions) and self-assessments to boost learners' reflection on their learning performance and actions. These strategies can inform the student about the skills they need to improve or to acquire. Also, the use of innovative tools like technological applications and software can engage the learners by accessing different types of materials that are tailored to their time and learning capabilities. In this case study, the designer could provide innovative learning by hosting many types of resources like exploring websites, videos, readings, and podcasts to enhance their engagement and give them the chance to choose the media they prefer. The same platform allows the instructor to create conversational situations like forums and messages and gives time for in-classroom debates in face-to-face sessions to acquire higher thinking skills.

Establishing flipped classroom needs to apply to the smart learning model principles that aim to transform any traditional learning to a smart and innovative one. However, it is not easy to explain to the teachers how to shift their jobs from a traditional classroom to blended learning, whatever is the combination chosen by the school, unless we give a clear and mapped explanation with specific details that we call the framework or model for learning.

As the university wishes to keep running face-to-face sessions, it is never stressed enough to say classroom sessions should be redesigned to suit the new flipped-classroom approach, as this is what we call best practices of eLearning. To do so, the designer has to implement the smart learning model and apply the following principles:

a. *Flexibility*: Implementing smart learning will need some arrangements that the instructional designer should conduct, like visit the classrooms and make sure that the new changes will allow flexible learning by using smart boards, projectors, laptops, or tablets and the usage of movable chairs and large tables placed in a way that allows brainstorming and collaboration requirements.

b. *Adaptability*: The instructional designer will need to allow for some furniture or helpful material that inclusion students may need. The adaptability is applied to the varied types of students and to the needs of the instructors to be able to guide all their students according to their special requirements.

c. *Comfort*: Provide a comfortable space to include extra furniture that allows the students to study in a comfortable way, like adding bean bags to the library, carpets, no-shoes spaces, and reading corners to give to the learner helpful design for individual and collaborative learning.

d. *Multiplicity*: The instructional designer will need to provide ideas about how to enhance creativity and critical thinking through a smart classroom design, from the types of decoration, the spaces provided to the learner, the discourse of the brainstorming, and the ability to access any information easily and quickly to keep the motivation of the students at a higher level.

e. *Connectivity*: The instructional designer should provide internet connectivity and individual devices as basic requirements to keep the learners connected to their learning platforms, to their notes and work, and to conduct social connectivity (social media) as part of the course to enhance the learning outcome of the students while interacting in different ways with peers inside and outside the classroom. The classroom environment must provide possible connectivity of the instructor and the learner in virtual learning platforms to improve the students' participation through the usage of LinkedIn, for instance, or Facebook as social learning experiences.

f. *Personalization*: The instructional designer must include activities that can enhance the learning environment and make it personalized to the learners themselves by conducting hands-on activities that can be displayed in the classroom progressively or projects that they can build progressively while they are in the classroom setting. The designer can extend the projects into artifacts that the student can achieve as an authentic assessment strategy for the flipped classroom. It starts with a theoretical vision in the virtual space, the LMS, then it extends to the classroom practice and then goes back to the application and integration in the virtual space for learning where the student can use advanced technological tools, software, and applications to achieve his artifact.

g. *Organization*: Activities should be designed in a way that allows self-learning, and to achieve it, the organization of the learning environment should be guided by the instructor to help the students discover gradually their learning process. After any activity, the furniture, stencils, or devices must be arranged in a way that will help the learner start his next activity. That is what class teachers do in a classroom setting. Let's take this good practice to the virtual learning space, where the student must find his content well-organized, displayed in a coherent way that helps him understand the course structure and to achieve his tasks with the minimum of hassle. Smart learning is related to technological tools; this is why extra devices should be allocated in a specific place to allow the students to keep working even when they forgot their own devices. The workflow in the LMS should be explained at the beginning of the course to explain to the learner what is expected from him to do each week and how. The objectives for each week should be displayed at the beginning, and the topics (modules) should be consistent throughout the learning and the design.

h. *Openness*: This is to explain that the classroom is not the only space where learning happens and where the instructor is considered the only source of the information. Virtual sources can be provided inside and outside the classroom in the school premises if necessary too and outside the LMS used. The instructor is a guide and coach for the students and can allocate many sources from where students can learn according to their interests, time, and place.

i. *Safety*: Accessing information with technological tools and devices will need to provide the learners a higher level of security to be able to work in a safe virtual environment. The instructional designer will need to integrate learning objectives where the students can understand the hazards of using technology while learning.

4. Innovative Application and Design

An innovative ID is to upgrade the student-learning journey in a way that makes it controllable and flexible at the same time through technology. The innovation process was taught at Stanford University (2017) for the purpose of providing the instructional designers with potentials that help them innovate in many ways while constructing their designs. The university used four stages that are considered the major steps in innovative-design thinking, which are as follows:

a. *Empathize*: In this first step, the designer should know the behavior of the learners closely using several technics: listening to them, observing and engaging with them in conversations to understand exactly what they need, how they learn, and how they think, then to allocate a degree of engagement that will help the designer select the right strategies for learning. Knowing the audience is the most important step to plan for instruction and define the learning outcomes and strategies to be used.

b. *Define*: To define is to bring clarity about the targeted learners. From empathizing mode, the designer could collect information about the learners, and now, he needs to create the right connection between the users and the needs. To find the challenging solutions for the type of learners he designs for, brainstorming with the design team will be the ideal technique to get the best solutions for the learners.

c. *Ideate*: This is a mental process of creating an idea that will be the fuel of the design by combining concepts to create solutions that work. In this step, the designer will need to step out of the obvious solutions to fall into creative ones. He needs to allocate potential unexpected solutions for his learners that will engage them to learn and cover the gaps he could allocate from the "define" stage. Some of the techniques used here are mind-mapping and sketching. These are cognitive approaches that could help the designer combine many learning theories with their application to come out with a new design for the audience of his project. The designer can incorporate as much technology as needed and try to locate new software and innovative ideas to implement the standards of eLearning instead of repeating what was done by the others in this field.

d. *Prototype*: Once the idea is generated, the designer will have to create a prototype or an artifact to represent cheaply and quickly his ideas and seek for feedback from the stakeholders who might interfere in some way for possible changes and to share the instructional design with a sample audience for testing, looking for potential bugs or problems in the instruction and to incorporate the users' needs and wants in his final version of the instruction.

e. *Test*: at this final stage of design thinking, the designer will redefine his prototype according to the feedback he could collect, and the testing of the artifact. More empathy for the learners' needs and wants will be built to help create stronger and more personalized solutions for them.

In this research, the designer could create innovative learning for his audience by changing the usual learning classroom and teacher-centered learning into student-centered and self-directed learning. This strategy is not really new in the world, but it is new for the learners of Indonesia, according to the faculty team who worked closely on this instruction. This shift could engage the learners to improve their outcome and motivate those who used to find the old teaching methods boring and monotonous. It gave to the students an opportunity to open up to new learning techniques and get involved in twentieth-century learning.

5. Creativity in Smart Learning

Some artists claim that Pablo Picasso, when he could not arise to the painting standards of his time, made a new scale that matches his abilities, and that's what made him stand out from the crowd.

Designing creative environments for learning might need to break some rules to provide innovative ideas to your students, and new ideas are always welcomed when it is about technology and virtual environment. Students like to discover new tools, apps, and software; and they like to change the way they are learning from time to time, as it keeps them engaged and motivated. To foster creativity in your instruction, it is important to create situations where students can investigate practical situations, and to enhance it, you need to find the right technology that encourage creativity.

Creativity can be reached by using cognitive and emotional functioning as developed by Alex Osborn (the father of brainstorming) and Sidney Parnes in the 1960s (Chant et al., 2009). It is to encourage critical thinking among the students and encourage them to solve problems in different ways from what is expected. This can't be achieved without creating scenarios from real-life problems, brainstorming the situations, and encouraging competition.

Instructional designers should understand that creativity is a skill that anyone can learn if given through small bites or smaller skills. Osborn-Parnes' creative problem-solving model (prepared by Parnes in 1981) provides a way to implement creativity in learning.

- Identify the goals or the challenges.
- Gather relevant facts and data.
- Clarify the challenge faced.
- Generate ideas.
- Converging ideas into a list to find main ideas.

- Refine these ideas to create action plan.

This model of work can implement creative thinking in students' work and can be used as a pattern in students' projects.

In the case study, in this section, we are relying on the instructional designer who hosted his course on Schoology as an innovative application for his audience. To understand how much this platform is helpful in providing transformative learning, it is important to look at the structure of the LMS.

In this case, the instructors can easily organize their course the way they consider effective for the learner. It allows grading, messaging, and badging the student. It is clear and fast in processing (opening, uploading, and downloading the documents). It can allow embedded videos and links to external resources that the university uses frequently. The instructor can post events and quizzes and keep his learners informed with messages and notifications.

6. Innovative Applications of Smart Learning

Smart education is a concept that emerged with the expansion of technological tools connected to the internet (Chan, 2002). Smart education programs were implemented all over the world gradually to facilitate learning. According to the website of UAE Ministry of Education, the United Arab Emirates launched its first experience in 2012 through a program called Mohamed Bin Rachid Smart Learning Program (MBRSLP). The program aims to implement smart learning initiatives and to develop the abilities of other countries to implement it based on their leading experience in the region. In this context, the program is stressing on the importance of the technology and communication that empowers and develops the educational process and improves it by bringing learning to the most deprived regions. All these reforms in education had specific purposes: to cover what the traditional learning could not effectively provide; to make learning reachable by a wider public anytime, anywhere; and to improve communication, collaboration, and constructive learning (Daniel, 2012).

Smart learning could be effective in many ways before and after COVID-19; it could realize the social distancing and provide personalized learning at the same time. However, using ubiquitous tools does not necessarily mean that the learners are having effective learning. Kim et al. (2013) consider that smart learning should be effective learning combined with social learning and ubiquitous education instead of being focused on using smart devices only, while Lee et al. (2014) consider that smart learning features are more than that, including the possibility of offering formal and informal learning, personalized content, and situated learning for people that are dispersed, and having the chance to connect people through collaborative learning experiences and social networks. They find that this feature of smart learning is the most important feature that any learning had to offer until now in the history of humanity.

Let us go back to the case study we're decorticating where we can see another feature of smart learning: flipped-classroom approach can allow learning to happen spontaneously without pressure or stress on the content or the learner. The student can choose his learning content from the list of contents offered by the instructor or just try to find new content from the internet. The guidance is the most important role of the instructor, as this can help in improving motivation and self-directed learning. The platform that was chosen by the instructional designer also offers a messaging service that works for mobile and e-mail notifications. Even a primary school learner can efficiently work and learn alone from this platform, and the instructor can receive updates on the quizzes and assignments submitted.

At the classroom session, the students could effectively conduct collaborative learning and brainstorm with discussions and debates with their peers the activities that they solved on the platform individually. This way, the instructional design could achieve the learning goals set for this project.

COVID-19 Back to School Arrangements

In the occasion of the flipped-classroom and blended-learning implementations that are taking effect in this time of the year of 2020, and with the preparation to seeing children getting back to their school premises, it is the right time to highlight the role of smart learning and instructional designers in conducting this generation to safe learning during the pandemic.

We explained in this chapter the implications of introducing flipped learning with smart applications to college students. And now, we need to stress on the same features of flipped and smart learning in this critical period. We need to visualize how the learning is going to be conducted across the UAE as a driving experience for many other countries in the region and around the world.

From an instructional design perspective, all schools have their prototype tested at the third term of the last academic year, which is a huge step to put aside, and to move further with the instruction. All schools already know the defects and the successes of their online-learning experience with their audience, and what needs to be done now is how to flip the learning and make it work with all the combinations that the KHDA (Knowledge and Human Development Authority) had proposed for the schools:

- Students will be present at the school premises for a full-time school day.
- Students will have to be at the school premises for a half school day only.
- Students will attend for just two days per week.
- Students will have face-to-face sessions every two weeks, against two weeks of online learning.
- Students will have to attend for two days the first week and three days for the next week, while they will get in the rest of the days online learning from home.

All these combinations displayed above are blended learning with a flipped-classroom approach.

Flipped classroom, as explained at the beginning of this chapter, is when students learn the lesson online and practice their learning in a classroom setting. It is self-directed learning with two approaches: pedagogical and andragogical approach, which must be combined in harmony to be able to extend learning into the students' homes in an organized and structured way.

The flipped-learning model reduces teacher-centered learning, and students are well involved with the content as they are invited to understand the topic before the face-to-face sessions, which gives the teacher a classroom full of ideas that the students constructed during their home learning and creates a rich field for discussions. This particular detail was noticeable during the last school term where students could come to the sessions with considerable knowledge of the topic, and they could share their math strategies and readings with their peers and teachers in the synchronous sessions. It also maximizes the in-class learning time, as the content is already available to the students on their school platforms.

Instructional designers can combine pedagogy and andragogy for UAE schools using the theories elaborated in chapter 1. Each theory will have an impact on the learning process and will help the instructional designer balance his strategies with the learning outcomes. On the other hand, they need to include a step-by-step strategy for the teachers to clarify how they will flip their classrooms according to Faculty Innovation Center at the University of Texas at Austin:

STEP 1 | Instructors need to identify what is the most important activity students can achieve in the classroom to demonstrate their skills and abilities and reveal their gap in learning. Besides, they need to allocate the topics that most students struggle with during the assessments, based on previous results, and to allocate the concepts where the instructor's guidance is a must.

STEP 2 | Instructors must dig deep into how to engage their students in face-to-face sessions with valuable feedback during the activities and applications. It is also necessary to understand how to engage them in an effective evidence-based instructional approach by leveraging collaboration and problem-based learning with peer feedback to find out what was easy and what was difficult in the topic to learn. This will solve some misconceptions and eliminate confusion that the students might have from self-learning.

STEP 3 | Instructors must define the learning goals for each session and know what are the exact practices to apply in face-to-face sessions that will prepare the students for the larger assignment posted online, taking into consideration that the students must get the connection between what is happening online and what they are practicing in the classroom. They also need to access a range of resources that will help them gain knowledge according to what they find comfortable for their learning and time. Consequently, the choice of the resources and tools to represent the content must help them manage the workload before and after the face-to-face class.

STEP 4 | Adapting the material of the course is to build balanced online resources and an organized environment for learning that will prepare the students for the acquisition of learning as we expect them to come prepared for the face-to-face session. To do so, it is important to know what is needed for reading, what is needed for skill-building, and what is required for the testing. Strategies and tools might vary from one platform to another, but what matters is to know how our students learn, and that is the role of the instructional designer who must gather information at the testing of the methodology for learning that was conducted earlier this academic year (2020). However, knowing what the student needs to view in a video presentation and what to read from a book chapter, a PDF, or a textbook will reduce the cognitive load as it will chunk the content into small objectives. The instructor must prepare his course to grow harder: keep the platform and the learning objectives simple at the beginning of the semester then increase gradually the learning objectives, and the content will increase for the learners. Some K-12 classes will require the integration of a forum where the instructor will ask a critical question that will guide the students to read more or to explore more resources to be able to answer the forum question. The instructor might also encourage interaction between the students in the forums by asking his students to comment on their peers' answers with questions or building on their ideas. Whatever is the strategy followed, the instructor must provide the learner with a PowerPoint presentation or a PDF where he gathers all the content of the session as a roadmap for the student, a palpable content to use for revision purposes.

STEP 5 | Instructors must provide a chance for their students to extend their learning by providing projects, quizzes, or assignments that invite the student to search for more resources outside his learning platform to be able to deepen his knowledge in the topic in question. Discussion boards, social media, additional readings about what was practiced in face-to-face sessions, LMS forums, and wikis are some ideas for inviting students to deepen their understanding and gain mastery.

Students' grade level might represent an obstacle in conducting an effective flipped classroom, especially for students with determination. Parents might not be able to deal with their child's disability and feel overwhelmed with the amount of work and time they need to spend with one of their children. To cover this gap, the instruction might allow for extra synchronous sessions providing to the elementary disabled students the right guidance, one-on-one teaching sessions, or even expanding the in-class time by designing some extra activities with the SEND teacher. Another instance that the parent might find frustrating and that the instructional designer should review constantly with the instructor is the type of resources and materials students with determination might struggle with, and explore alternatives for the instructor to facilitate the student's interaction with the content. Some applications and software look very easy to use by any child, while in fact, they represent a challenge for students with a certain disability. Parents' feedback can help understand how their child can finish his work faster and submit his assignment online in a way that reflects the efforts deployed by his own. However, flipped classroom requires a certain level of self-learning; it is important, though, to keep up the same features and challenges for all students: if the child cannot conduct self-learning in the way we present it to him, it is time for the instructional designer to find another solution, another platform, with other resources or tools! Constant evaluation of the processes is a must to achieve successful learning at all times.

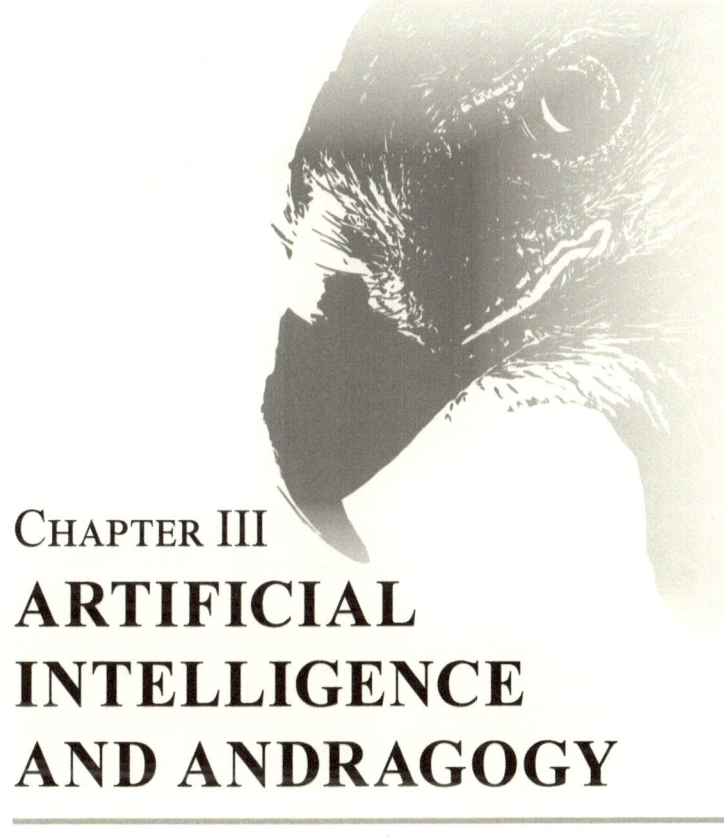

Chapter III

ARTIFICIAL INTELLIGENCE AND ANDRAGOGY

1. Adult Learning and Artificial Intelligence

Exploring adult learning supervised by technologies can construct stronger relationship in organizations, communities of practices and adult learning in schools. To understand how we can combine artificial intelligence (AI) with collective intelligence (CI) to enhance the learning experience of the adult learner, we're going to design a combination that explains how AI can work better when it is collecting data from a group of individuals than from separated individuals.

General AI is usually confounded with narrow AI. General AI is the technology that can achieve at the level of human intelligence, which is a futuristic technology that we do not reach yet, while narrow or weak AI is a technology that exists and can cover some specific human activities like examining a student or solving some problems or tasks in a limited or defined situation.

In this section, we will be using AI as an indication to the narrow AI. We will discover how people are connected through data collection and search engines rather than through e-mails, workplaces, or conferences. We will discuss how the strategy of connecting people works more effectively when it is based on a huge data collection, and we will explain the relationship between crowdsourcing and AI usage to enhance collective intelligence. This shift from the humanitarian approach to automatic approach is developing our relationship from random to carefully selected by going from simple automaticity to a wider and smarter interaction between human and machines. Then, we will explore the effective AI design, techniques, and uses in organizations; we will discuss the game theory, crowdsourcing, and collective intelligence by answering the following question: *How can we use the powers of AI to build quality collective intelligence and improve adult learning experience?*

The knowledge management that is happening in different organizations and communities is connecting people to extract from their shared and collective experiences the knowledge economy needed to build collective intelligence.

2. Collective Intelligence (CI)

Collective intelligence is an expression that is defined in different ways. Levy's definition (1994) seems here the most appropriate for what we're going to be elaborated further ahead. He defines it as *"a form of universally distributed intelligence, constantly enhanced, coordinated in real time, and resulting in the effective mobilization of skills."* And if we want to explain CI in an easier way, we will say that observing a colony of ants can give us more details about how ants are behaving than if we observe only one ant, and that is how organizations are observed to understand the collective intelligence of the members (Malone and Bernstein, 2015, p.39).

Malone, Laubacher, and Dellaroccos (2010) tried to study the collective intelligence of people by using the common patterns that the internet is providing through different disciplines and platforms to connect human intelligence. What they found was extraordinary important: collective intelligence is a set of information they called CI genes, and that is collected by answering the following questions:

- o What is being done? (Create and Decide)
- o Who is doing it? (Hierarchy and Crowd)
- o Why are they doing it? (Motivation and Glory)
- o How is it being done? (Collaboration and Group Decision)

These questions of the CI genes will be our building blocks to understand how AI can collect these bits of intelligence as data to manage different electronic communities and informal organizations.

Jeopardy! is an American show where the players must compete by answering quiz questions very quickly. These questions are written in a very complex and rich language using ambiguities and references from thousands of domains. The players must have excellent language skills and be very accurate in all the domains. In 2007, IBM created a system using a DeepQA technology that competed in *Jeopardy!* (Ferrucci et al., 2012). They called it Watson. Watson played against *Jeopardy!* champions and won the game. The system was not using a database of questions and answers; it was using an analytical strategy that was doing the following steps:

- Gathering knowledge in different domains
- Evaluating the potential answers
- Collecting formal and informal language sources for that specific answer
- Searching the best answer that was linked to the best supporting evidence
- Counting the scoring result (computational intelligence)

Watson was not just finding the right answer but was also analyzing the answers of the players through evidence analysis to support or decline their answers. The key strategy it was using was related to the *"type, time, geography, popularity, passage support, source reliability, and semantic relatedness."* (Ferrucci et al., 2012), and these are the basic elements that human researchers use to accurate their studies and researches.

Watson is the AI that we are looking for to build smart communities of practices and organizations and link them all to a huge smart system to collect quality CI for each domain.

The smart system can feed itself with data to become smarter after every connection, word typing, and upload of a resource. And that is what is called crowdsourcing.

Croudsourcing is to collect the maximum information that one needs from the internet, social network, or from a group of connected people (Wikipedia), while collective intelligence is how accurate is the information we collected.

AI can play a strong role in enhancing CI and managing CoP at the same time. It can cover a range of roles in no time, to evaluate potentials and gather information from different platforms to give an accurate overview of the interests and study the actions of peoples from different perspectives, and the implication of people in some specific fields through their actions. But we cannot speak about crowdsourcing and AI without game theory.

3. Crowdsourcing, AI, and Game Theory

Game theory is a kind of mathematics that consists of studying the interaction between the parties in a game. It was used first in economics and then generalized to other fields of study to view the accuracy of the results and the utility of the application of the theory. It is used to *"express, study, and design the interaction between the promoter and the group of people"* (Estellés-Arolas, 2018).

Crowdsourcing is to gather individuals in an open platform to perform a task collaboratively (Estelles-Arolas, 2018). The initiative to claim crowdsourcing must include the following elements:

- *"A crowdsourcer that promotes the initiative;*
- *A specific task to be done with a clear objective;*
- *A crowd that will carry out that task;*
- *A reward to be given to the crowd in exchange for that task;*
- *A benefit to be perceived by the crowdsourcer for the execution of that task;*
- *A participative process that required a conscious activity by the crowd;*
- *An open call, so that anyone can participate;*
- *Internet as a means of interaction."*

If one of these eight elements is eliminated, the crowdsourcing will become something else.

Let's say that we are eliminating the conscious activity of the crowd. In this case, the crowdsourcing will become passive crowdsourcing, and the crowd is not answering to a call for a task consciously like to read and analyze the comments of people on Twitter to know who is winning the elections.

Crowdsourcing elements are also present in the game theory. Let's combine now these elements in a platform that is managed with AI. This latter will facilitate the interaction of the crowd and guide the members in a way that helps get better outcomes. The design of the platform is also important to build a meaningful experience.

And to have interaction beyond expectations, AI needs to perform beyond mediating and interacting between the machine and the crowd. AI should be performing in a way that facilitates the creation of a real community of practice. A community that is managed by AI to merge to its functions, the collective intelligence, and nurture itself to become more intelligent and thus powerful.

Communities of practices are now formed automatically based on each one's interests that can show up through the history of one's internet connection. AI tracks it all, can gather all information through evidence and resources. The information will generate data about everyone as an element in a society, then as an individual in a crowd.

4. AI Role in Building CI in Adult Dearning

AI can help collect collective intelligence while learning is occurring. We're going to discuss the design of this learning process through the CI genes that are the resource for providing information:

a. **Create and Decide:** In the first stage, the adult learner is facing a problem in his organization. He's going to search for a solution somewhere on the internet. While he's searching, the learner receives a notification that he is invited to join X or Y community, dealing with the problem of his research. Algorithms are the key here as they help machines to connect data and select the best option. The learner will have to choose then a community to join. Once he clicks on Accept, AI will help him build his profile from the data he has in his computer. And again, he needs to confirm the profile (another updated data for AI) to start receiving gradually important messages from the members of the community that are dealing closely with his research topic. The adult learner will evaluate which information is helpful to solve his problem and ends up by deciding on the right solution.

b. **Hierarchy and Crowd:** The crowd is important for AI to collect information and data. People around the world post websites, blogs, and resources; they create links, hashtags, and wikis. Then other people show their interests by liking, sharing, and commenting. All this information is linked together by algorithms to collect data on individuals. The crowd is building a collective intelligence that will be used by AI to connect each user to the right information he's looking for.

Hierarchy is very important for AI too. Hierarchy here means the importance of the resource according to the importance of the user. If you are a student and you are posting information, it will be classified as less important than the one posted by a specialist, a writer, or a researcher; and when AI calls for information, it selects according to the most relevant resource according to the intellectual hierarchy.

c. **Motivation and Glory:** Motivation is always an important element in building meaningful learning. Adult learners can be motivated by their professional growth or life change or even learning just to learn. However, AI is considered the unbeaten robot who is going to take human jobs, but in fact, AI, if used effectively, will have the greatest role in raising the level of the CI in organizations; and instead of doing the role of the human and free human from any obligations, AI can increase the level of CI by pushing people to solve higher-order problems. AI is not the only thing that is improving; the human workforce also is getting better skills. Using and encouraging to acquire new skills of the century is the best motivator for the adult learner. The objective of the learning will be now how to improve the quality of the production for sustainability and what kind of data to feed the machine and minimize the clutches and dysfunctions and improve productivity with fewer costs.

d. **Collaboration and Group Decision:** Collaboration was always the strength that lead to an effective learning. Now let's imagine that the whole world is only one community through AI. Eventually, in this case, there are no geographic limits, no differences in time zones, no language barriers, and no discrimination. AI can solve all these problems that once were considered a challenge to build stronger communities. Now, decisions are made based on Japanese resources; they are applied in a European organization located in Africa. The world is really getting better learning, and real collaboration is made through algorithms.

DESIGNING SCHOOL LEARNING WITH AI FUNCTIONS

Nowadays, the basic stone in knowledge management is collaborative work. AI can offer a range of services that are coherent and can contribute in building stronger communities in less time and fewer human effort through crowdsourcing (Weld et al., 2014).

The usage of AI for crowdsourcing can help increase the quality and flexibility of the learning and enhance the quality of collective intelligence. The adaptive learning techniques used by AI will help analyze the learner's work, style of learning, frequency of logins, resource sharing, and even their academic achievements and hobbies. These details will help, for example, to gather learners automatically who have different skills to work together on a specific assignment in schools in an optimal group formation.

AI can be the source of lots of information for the learner. If well designed, the machine can provide training to the learners and conduct it at any time, in any language, and on any subject matter the learners require. Having a virtual peer or instructor also can improve interaction and understanding and makes discussions more interesting for the learners as they will feel involved in a learning process that is progressing at their own pace and collaboratively at the same time. Besides, it is always exciting to have a knowledgeable peer to conduct a collaborative project or an assignment!

Instructors need constant help when they conduct synchronous course, webinar, or conference. AI, as a support instructor, can use adaptive technology to listen, analyse, and moderate the sessions, read learner's discussions, place them in a report, and deliver the organized session report accurately to the instructor from where the instructor can understand how much the learners are involved and how much benefit they get from the course.

AI moderator can also help in organizing the resources, videos, and dashboards of the learners. They can provide perfect delivery plan courses, and integrate into each course the information that the learner needs, in other words, to provide customized courses with personalized quizzes and assignments.

Artificial intelligence (AI) is a great approach to apply with collective intelligence to gain effective learning experiences. It has benefits as well as drawbacks that will be discussed further.

AI has a huge impact on learning with the advent of Web 2.0. This impact helped in collecting data, and AI is receiving from the internet tons of user information, which will be used to adapt the research of the internet users according to their interest. Once we use adaptive learning technique with AI technology, the following positive impact will appear. CoPs will be formed automatically according to the interest of the learners detected by the adaptive technique of AI. It reduces the time that people take to find communities that they are interested in and makes it an easy task. Since most of our daily tasks are repetitive, with AI, these tasks can be done automatically and easily.

In CoPs, AI can recognize the practical steps of forming communities, the strategies to run them, and the effective way to keep the learners or the members informed and motivated all the time. It is a repetitive work that needs no intelligence, but with AI, it is done with accuracy because all information about the members is stored and connected to the interest for everyone. Reports are more accurate, we have more information than before, gathered from one single community, including the problems they faced and the difficulties of each member in coping with the community; and learning is much better diffused, as the information can reach everybody now. AI can prepare the resources, conferences, and webinars and can conduct sessions through virtual presenters and speakers. It gathers all the required information to conduct a session. AI can collect information and resources in no time and expose them in the most beautiful way it could be, as it has all information about the members and their preferences, even the colors they prefer! The virtual speaker who plays the role of the expert has no time limit, can answer any question, and find any resource based on the most relevant resources and the most popular references of the subject. Virtual peers are created to engage the interaction with the human peer easily. To explain this point, I call for the football games or chess competitions with AI where the machine studies the moves of the human player to compete better and smarter. The positive impact of using AI will reflect on collective intelligence because the information is more accurate and better manipulated. The CI is accelerated by the effective learning that such platforms can provide to the adult learner.

However, AI has disadvantages even if these are less than the benefits. The learner and the collective intelligence can be affected in some points. By using AI, a huge displacement in human workforce will occur. Instructors are concerned experts will no longer be useful for human learners and most learning activities will be managed by AI. Computational intelligence (or the ability of a computer to learn a specific task from data or experimental observation [Wikipedia]) will do all the thinking instead of the human learner. The human learner might become again a passive learner sitting in front of the computer and getting his researches in his inbox. Addiction in getting AI services is making human services very simple-minded. We might end up living with a machine that "thinks" we are the weaker element, and instead of building our collective intelligence, it destroys it.

Designing smart and innovative learning is a huge step that needs to be planned, implemented, and frequently evaluated. In some situations, we design new instructions to create a shift in a paradigm that suit this era. And evaluation and reevaluation of the instruction can improve the performance of the design by bridging the gaps and building a homogeneous instruction for our learners.

In addition, instructional designers are supposed to recontextualize the curriculum and make it suitable for the learners according to what their future will require as skills and learning contexts. When we design for a futuristic perspective, we have to call for some skills that are not fully known today but should be taught, like introducing AI, which is an important concept to include in our curriculum when we think about designing a new one. First of all, we must think about how to incorporate new skills that the teacher might not have. In here, we will call for the *curriculum theory* (precisely engineering theories) where three processes are involved in the recontextualization of the curriculum:

- How to select knowledge?
- How to sequence it?
- How to pace it to the learners and the instructors' knowledge and practice?

The quality of predictions demonstrated through the selection of the curriculum components will allow the learner to connect what he is learning now to what he will practice in the future.

Incorporating AI in the curriculum system and programs should be focused on coding and robotics, and tools that teach the concepts of AI to guide students in their understanding of the twenty-first-century skills and to prepare them for their career success. These concepts are based on visual recognition; landmark-based navigation; manipulation of objects and robotics; facial recognition and expressions; speech recognition, including cultural traits; and speech generation, including linguistic differentiation.

There are some tools that the schools are already using to move toward AI generation like AI-in-a-Box, which is a course based on STEAM and project-based learning to teach key concepts of AI.

It also offers to the teachers courses to improve their skills while using this tool in their classrooms, to help them in teaching AI lessons about robotics engineering. Such tools can be useful in the implementation of a new curriculum based on new skills and can give the chance to the teachers to select the knowledge, sequence it, and pace it to the requirements of the curriculum in order to upgrade their courses and skills and be able to practice what the curriculum requires from them.

Smart applications can prepare our students to perform better in their unknown future, where nowadays learning might be unnecessary for them, as we cannot imagine the type of jobs they will occupy and the kind of environments they will work in. This is why we try to incorporate as much technology as we, instructional designers and teachers, can to give for better chances and closer insights to what they might need for their uncertain future.

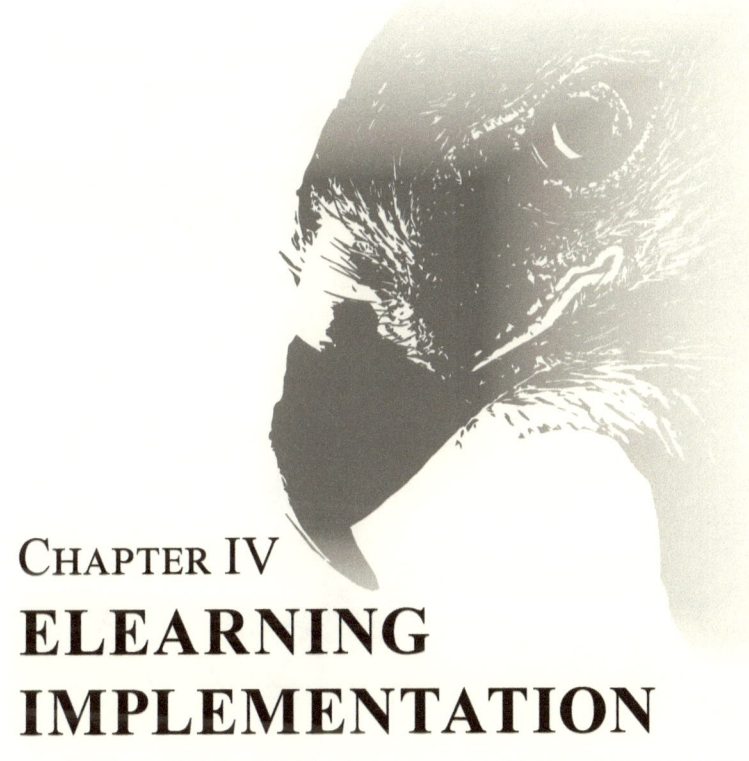

Chapter IV
ELEARNING IMPLEMENTATION

Introducing a new learning environment all of a sudden is a risky step. People tend to reject new experiences they were not prepared for. Similarly, introducing eLearning as an innovative step in schools needs preparation and good management skills.

In this chapter, we will explain how to introduce eLearning as an innovative strategy providing to the learners a new experience to reshape their educational performance. This step cannot be made without studying the change models that the school management needs to follow, and we will focus on several stages of the implementation process. These stages are explained via the usage of a certain model at each of them, then we will give explanations on how the model chosen for the given stage will worked at the school setting. We will explain why we have to consider many models of change instead of one. Then, we will categorize each model during the implementation of change management according to the school strategy of work. And to avoid the failures that one model can engender, we will explain how each model can cover each stage of the change. At the end, an overview will be given about the advantages and the disadvantages of the usage of these models during and after the implementation.

MODELS TO USE IN eLEARNING DRIVE TO CHANGE

There are several reasons why we need to introduce partial or radical change in our lives. It is mainly due to the fact that people and organizations evolve for several reasons according to the six theories of change that explain the insights of this process: evolutionary, teleological, life-cycle, dialectical, social-cognition, and cultural theory. This is why, there are several models of change, and each model is embedded under a category and is designed to cover certain specifications of the change process (Singh and Hardaker, 2017).

Being able to implement new strategies in an organization successfully means that the change process could give attention to all the stages effectively, which are understanding the change, planning the change, implementing the change, and communicating the change. These four stages will be the focus points in explaining the different models followed to implement a successful change process.

Theories of change help define why this chapter should be divided into change process stages, and each stage should have a specific model to follow. Therefore, we call here for several theories of change that are more social cognitive than systematic because change is about changing people's behavior and learning to unlearn to be able to learn something new (Azmi, 2008).

Lewin K. (1951) accredited his *field theory* and explained that all changes can be successful if an inner or outer motivation is established in the individuals. Another theory came to explain that Lewin's *field theory* is not enough to drive a successful change. We have to measure the readiness of the organization too, which goes beyond the individuals (Hox, 2010). At this level, we recall *McKinsey's Framework*, where the relationship between the individuals and the systems of the organization is also important to include in our plan for change.

Change efficacy is higher when the individuals share a collective goal for change (Bandura, 1986). The relationship can go further in a more systematic approach when finance, resources, and materials are included in the change process. Then we have theories of change applicable at the implementation, and during this stage, we need to make sure that the change is effective through a successful process. And here, we call for Kotter's model that describes the eight stages of a successful change management process (Buller, 2019). In the same reference, it is stated that one of the principles of change is to combine models in order to cover the gaps found within one model.

UNDERSTANDING THE CHANGE

With the spread of the pandemic, it became necessary to incorporate changes in all work settings around the country, including schools, and eLearning seems to be the right choice to keep control of the learning and the health of our students and academics.

It is true that this change will create new opportunities for those who are involved and build new skills for students, parents, and academics. However, this sudden shift could be smoother if well studied and designed according to the theories of change. School leaderships decided to incorporate eLearning according to the requirements of the situation and the Ministry of Education. But let's look in detail how to prepare a school for such a transition if we had a choice to do it smoothly. Any school leadership must understand first that the eLearning change process will affect the school on two important layers: *organizational change* and *pedagogical change*. Then they will need to define strategies needed to implement to perform a smooth and effective change. To understand how to initiate the change process, it is important to break down the steps using *Lewin's model of change*. In the following infographic, we describe the three steps for change management.

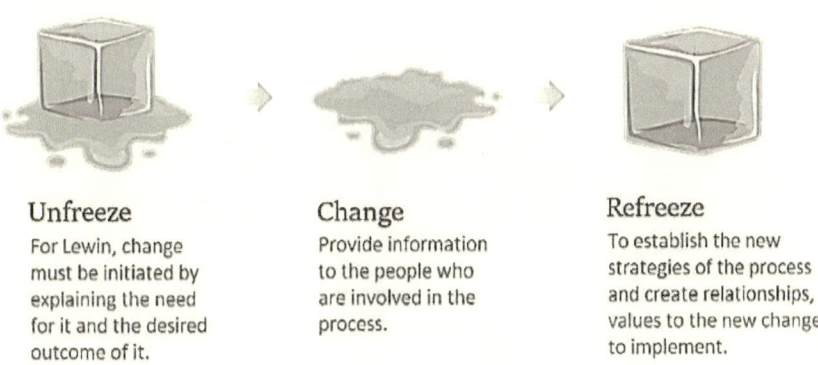

Unfreeze

For Lewin, change must be initiated by explaining the need for it and the desired outcome of it.

Change

Provide information to the people who are involved in the process.

Refreeze

To establish the new strategies of the process and create relationships, values to the new change to implement.

Figure 4. The three steps of Lewin's model of change.

The common tool to use for *Lewin's model* of change is communication and motivation. It helps give first an overview of the change that the leadership is going to implement.

Expanding the school services by implementing eLearning for the different departments will need to create trust between the community of learners and the instructors who are new to this type of learning. Following Lewin's model of change will reduce the uncertainty of the learners in question and increase motivation by giving enough details like how to conduct the sessions, how to receive material, what the basic requirements of the learners are, and what the instructors need to have in order to be considered apt for the change. And if these basic requirements are not found, how does the school prepare the instructors and the learners to become effective during and after the implementation of the eLearning?

PLANNING FOR CHANGE

Planning for change is one of the most important stages where the leadership will need to evaluate the organization to understand how much the change is needed and how much the organization will be effective after the change. To do so, a holistic approach should be followed (McKinsey, 2008). The school leadership can choose the *McKinsey 7S Framework* to plan for the change.

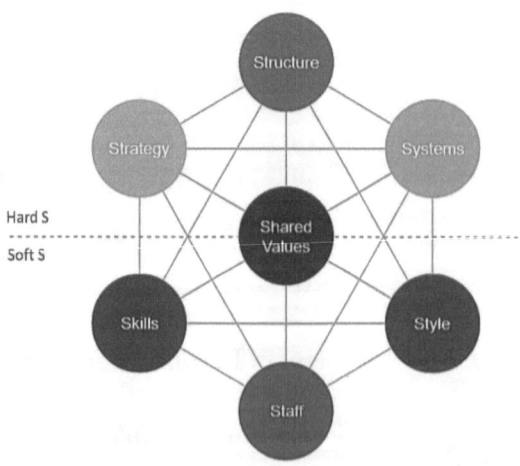

Figure 5. McKinsey 7S framework for planning change management.

The framework will help the management understand the relationship between the different elements of the school and collecting information that could be effective in making any change, like including new services and staff and determining which skills the eLearning will require to plan for the training of the staff; and communicate this information to all stakeholders, students, instructors, and parents, or delegating some instructors or employees with good communication skills to communicate the change requirements. By going through this framework, leadership will reduce the gap in implementing the new eLearning strategies.

IMPLEMENTING THE CHANGE

Applying change is a fact, and making it a long-term effective change is another fact. The implementation of change will not be successful unless it shows long-term effectiveness. It is true that the implementation will need structural planning as we explained earlier, but good planning cannot be sustained if the implementation is not done in the right way (Steven, 2012). To be sure that this stage is well covered, the leadership will need to follow another model than the one used for implementation. We call here for *John Kotter's eight steps to successful change.*

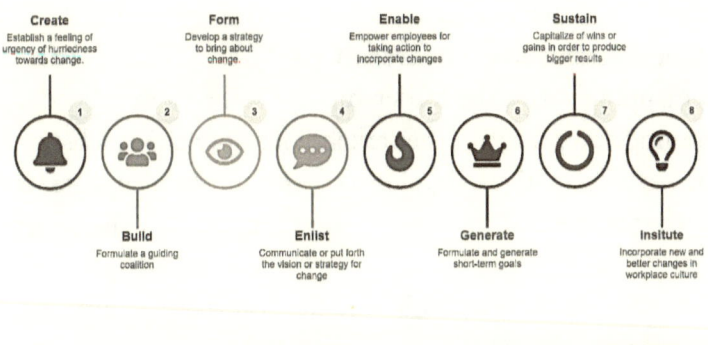

Figure 6. Kotter's eight steps to successful change. Retrieved form https://medium.com/@warren2lynch/a-comprehensive-guide-to-kotters-8-step-model-of-change-43d4eb86f1ea

After planning for change, the leadership will try to implement eLearning pilot test and urge students, teachers, parents, and administrators to be part of it. The instructors and the students chosen for the pilot test will be the guiding coalition used to help other students and other instructors understand the applied strategy of the school. The pilot test group will share their experience with the other instructors and students who will be more open-minded to receive comments from people of their social range about the new change. The coalition will grow then by communication. The pilot test will show the gaps in the system and will highlight the technical and physical failures of the implementation. This will help the leadership improve the eLearning experience to make it sustainable, show that the situation is under control to create trust, and perform an effective and successful change.

COMMUNICATING THE CHANGE

To communicate the change to the stakeholders, it is important to start mapping the communication. From the beginning of the project, the leadership must brainstorm the situation, including facts, statistics, and proofs that change is needed. Identifying the stakeholder's needs is also important to cover all their requirements and then map the communication according to their financial involvement, influences, and learning abilities (Walker et al., 2008). In the mapping stage, the leadership can follow a matrix of work by determining and prioritize the stakeholders, preparing a list of names and their representatives, develop a communication engagement plan for the change needed, execute it, and then monitor the progress for change.

This will help the leadership find the best way to communicate the change steps and process the gaps found and the final implementation results. The adoption of new strategies is an innovative step to consider from time to time to evolve through change. However, providing a good understanding of the need to change, a perfect planning, and a soft implementation can build a good scaffolding for this constructive methodology. This scaffolding can be made by communication and building relationships between the different components of the organization. It opens the individuals to a new learning journey and can create perfect changemakers.

As explained earlier in this chapter, the models that we can use to implement eLearning in schools are complementary. The chosen models can provide a balanced implementation process of change management. During the implementation, the leadership might notice the following positive impact on the environment of the school and the individuals:

- The instructors are getting important training that will help them reshape their own experiences and gain twenty-first-century skills. *Lewin's model* can help implement good communication with the individuals inside the school.

- A new relationship between the leadership vision and the need for change is emerging, which might be a source for extra income to the school through the new eLearning courses. And here we call for *McKinsey's model*, which provides connections between the different elements of the organization.

- The school environment is going to be refreshed by the innovative eLearning strategy as many meetings, discussions, and workshops are held with both students and instructors to help them cope with the new situation. *Lewin's model* can help the school define, in the refreezing stage, the structures that support the new strategies of work (Buller, 2019).

- Conducting a pilot test might promote collective learning for change and involve individuals in the new identity of the school department.

- The stakeholders will see the need to communicate the change to the parents who need to be informed by their new role in the change process and how they can sustain their children for the new eLearning journey. Here we call for *Lewin's model* (Buller, 2019).

- All school departments and sections must be aware of the new vision that the school is trying to create through the innovative change of eLearning. We call here for *Kotter's model* where the school leadership will develop a shared vision.

After the implementation, the school leadership might detect some failures during the implementation of the eLearning. This failure is considered a gap that any procedure could skip unintendedly. This can be explained by the usage of the wrong model for change as each model serves a situation and fails in another. For example, Kotter's change model is made to encourage new behaviors for successful organizational change while Prosci ADKAR model rewards individual change and aims to implement awareness at the level of the individuals inside the organization. Some other models target the stakeholders and leadership response to change while few others aim to combat emotional resistance like Lewin's Model. Choosing the right combination of models can balance the procedure and make it effective for the organization.

However, the following points are about the disadvantages that the school might notice after the implementation:

- After the implementation, more training might be required for the instructors, and a bigger IT team might be needed to support the new learning system. These requirements might make a slight disbalance in finance. We call here for the first stage: understanding the change, where the leadership might not specify in detail what to change and what to deploy in order to have a better result of change. This might be due to *Lewin's model*, as it does not provide details on how to prepare exactly for change.
- Other problems might emerge at the pilot test stage, which are gaps that any change can engender at this stage. These defects need to be resolved for an effective final implementation.

CHAPTER V
PROGRAM
PLANNING &
EVALUATION

Planning and Evaluation

Program planning is a development process that coordinates and facilitates change according to a need or a defined problem, while program evaluation is a conclusive step that measures the desirable quality of plans and programs. In an ideal research world, evaluations are carried out perfectly, and the results are useful and valuable. Unfortunately, when it comes to performing evaluations in the real world, mistakes are made, details go awry, and challenges can seem insurmountable. Many challenges are considered guidelines for an evaluator to execute an effective evaluation, which are as follows:

1. *Poor planning:* Being unable to plan effectively or to deliver poor planning can affect the outcomes of the program, which is also the same thing for poor evaluation. It can affect the time scheduled for the delivery of the program and make the outcomes unclear. The same is going to happen to the resources like the funding and the personnel needed to accomplish the tasks and the timeframe of the evaluation itself.

2. *Lack of readiness:* If the participants are not ready for the evaluation, the participants will not cooperate in an effective way as well as the stakeholders. This situation can question the whole evaluation process: *Why do we need it?*

3. *Bad questions:* Deciding on the right questions to ask to get you the results you're looking for is a key element of the evaluation process. Asking the wrong questions can derail a project. What are bad questions? Unclear questions that use too much jargon, that don't consider the audience, that are biased in any way, and that don't have a clear and understandable method are considered problems for the process.

4. *Bad data:* If you don't properly and cleanly input the data you get, if there is missing, messy, or unorganized data, then the results will also be messy and unorganized and, ultimately, not useful.

5. *Too much data:* If the collection of data is not limited to a certain purpose, then the amount of the work to translate

the data will overlap the work needed. The data should be precise and concise; it needs to have a purpose, and it needs to be meaningful for the whole evaluation process.

6. *Ineffective approaches:* If you don't use the right data-collection methods, you don't understand how to properly and correctly identify data, you don't have a thorough understanding of outputs and outcomes, and/or you don't choose the right evaluator for your project, then you won't have an effective or positive evaluation experience.

Evaluation is a systematic method for collecting, analyzing, and using data to examine the effectiveness and efficiency of programs and, as importantly, to contribute to continuous program improvement (Diamond, 2013). There are many forces for change that call for planning and evaluating an online program, and the most relevant reasons for conducting any type of evaluation are the following:

1. *Expanding the program:* We need to plan and evaluate an existing program in case we needed to expand it through collaboration or partnership with other universities, colleges, or schools, or through the expansion of the program inside the same organization by opening new branches or departments or including new rules or delivery methods to the students.

2. *Bridging the gaps:* Online learning always creates gaps in time and space between students and course development and delivery. Prioritizing the flexibility and connection in online learning needs planning and evaluation.

3. *Integrity in online testing:* Online testing comes with challenges from technology, policy, and budget requirements. This is why we need to plan for an evaluation system to rectify or review the policies, and/or integrate new technology that will create unbalance in budgeting.

4. *Third-party partnership:* This is to take into consideration the cost and other benefits and pitfalls of the program planning,

including the online resources and the platform needed to accomplish the task of the evaluator.

5. *Technology integration:* Integrating new technology to a teaching program may need an evaluation to assess the learning outcomes and the delivery of the instruction.

6. *Innovation in teaching strategies:* To innovate the teaching strategies and implement new ones for an online course or change the syllabus or the program, we need to evaluate the program and plan for the integration of new strategies.

7. *Impact of the program:* Online programs may need an evaluation at the end of their application to assess the effective outcome from the program after some time of running it.

PROACTIVE RISK ASSESSMENT

The next step in planning and evaluation is to consider what the risks are that we're going to face during the evaluation process of our program. Under this title, we're going to carry out a *proactive risk assessment* or *preliminary risk assessment* (PRA). It is the easiest way to assess risks and a great method to use at the planning stage. It goes in the following logical steps:

STEP 1	STEP 2	STEP 3	STEP 4	STEP 5
DETERMINE THE HAZARD OR THE UNWANTED EVENT	FIND THE HARM OR CONSEQUENCES.	DETERMINE THE POTENTIAL CAUSES.	DETERMINE THE SEVERITY AND CONSEQUENCE	DETERMINE THE POSSIBLE ADDITIONAL CONTROLS OR ACTIONS
What could go wrong?	What might be the potential impact?	How might the hazard occur?	What is the likelihood the hazard and the harm will occur (rating scale)? How significant is the impact? Calculate the risk score from the risk matrix.	What might control or mitigate the hazard?
EXAMPLE IN ONLINE EDUCATION	EXAMPLE IN ONLINE EDUCATION	EXAMPLE IN ONLINE EDUCATION	EXAMPLE IN ONLINE EDUCATION	EXAMPLE IN ONLINE EDUCATION
The LMS fails to open.	Students cannot access the material.	When there are many students online.	Rating score can be high, medium or low according to the risk matrix.	Reschedule the courses according to the number of students allowed to show online at the same time.

Figure 7. Proactive risk assessment steps.

Theory of Change

The *theory of change* is a methodology that aims to plan and evaluate programs to promote social change. It defines the goals of a specific program then maps the evaluation according to the shorter-term, intermediate, and longer-term 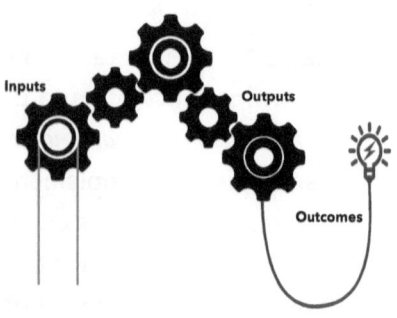 outcomes. The relationship between the actual outcomes and the desired outcomes can map the evaluation requirements and explain the necessary intervention to achieve and, consequently, to plan. As we follow the steps for designing or revising a course, a curriculum, or a program, it is extremely important to keep in mind the relationship that remains constant whether we are focusing on a curriculum, a course, a unit, or a part within a program. To do so, we need to follow the *logic model* process. It allows any evaluator to keep this relationship standing in a coherent visual representation of all the necessary parts of his program evaluation.

Logic Model

Logic model, also called a *conceptual model*, is a visual representation to design, plan, and evaluate a program or a course. It shows the different parts of the program and how each part is related to another to reach the intended outcomes. It is a cause-and-effect process that shows how the activities will flow together to achieve program outcomes.

Table 3 represents a logic model designed to evaluate the usage of critical thinking in a course. The different parts of the model can be built by asking questions at each part:

a. *Objectives:* To find the objectives, we need to ask ourselves, *What are we trying to achieve?*

b. *Success and verification measures:* To find the success measures and the verification of these measures, we need to ask ourselves, *How we're going to measure it?*

c. *Assumptions:* To find the assumptions, we need to ask, *What other conditions must exist?*

d. *Inputs:* To find the inputs, we need to ask ourselves, *How do we get there?*

Figure 8. Logic model process.

Once we've made the visual representation of our program or course, we process the different parts and evaluate the relationship between each part with its related section according to the questions we used to fill in the table. The orange arrows create the relationship starting from the inputs until we reach the goals set at the beginning, and that's how the theory of change works: it connects the different parts of the model to reach the goals.

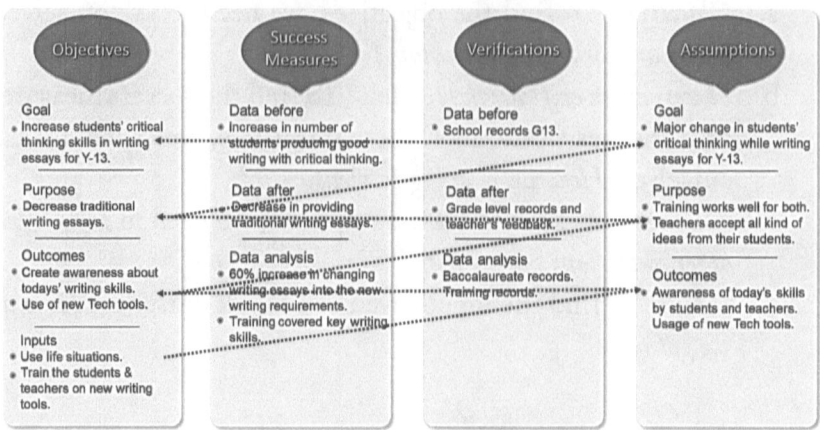

Figure 9. Building relationships in the logic model.

SOFT SYSTEMS MODEL

The soft systems model (SSM) is an evaluation approach developed by Peter Checkland from the University of Lancaster. The word *systems* here refers to "the problem to be found" related to the individuals and to be readdressed by this approach, which might be a confusing element for all participants and might be a source of debate if mentioned before the evaluation. That is why it is kept unknown. This model seeks to explore problematic situations caused by human activities. It aims to break down peoples' minds and perceptions to find the problem in a messy situation and understand the context in which the system functions (Yadin, 2013). The soft systems model goes through seven steps of verification of the process to understand what is going wrong.

The SSM evaluation approach is usually applied when we need to to identify the problem and try to resolve the different and source of conflict point of views of the stakeholders or the managers to be able to allocate the main reason for failure of the learning program. And to be able to identify the different contributor to the creation of a conflict situation, SSM has a methodology to process the contributors who require analysis. The contributors are represented by the mnemonic

CATWOE: the customer, the actors, the transformation process, the worldview, the owner, and the environmental constraints. According to the seven stages of SSM, we develop our CATWOE.

Stage 1 and 2 are mainly set to define the problem and to describe the problematic situation. *Stage 3* is where basic definitions are captured in the system thinking. In *stage 4*, we define the activities of the instruction using action verbs and the interconnection between these activities and the main goals set for the training or the program. In *stage 5*, we can compare the real-world application and its relevance with the systems (the conceptual models). It is to compare what actually happened in our eLearning with what is supposed to happen. *Stage 6* is to try to debate and communicate to find out how to improve the situation. *Stage 7* is to define how to apply the changes to improve the new cycle of eLearning.

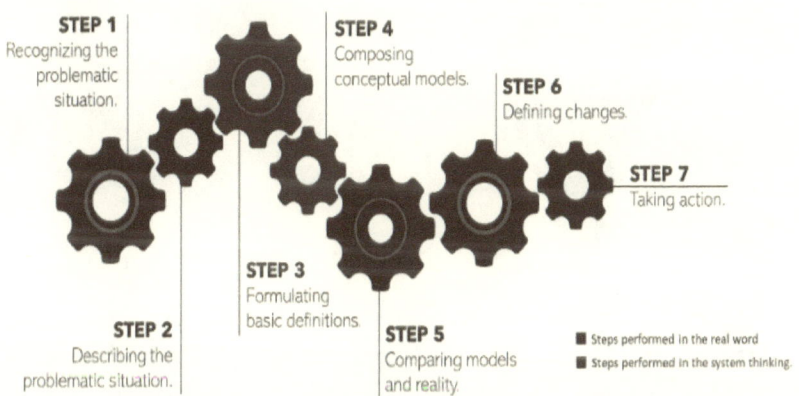

Figure 10. Seven Steps of the soft systems model for program evaluation.

KIRKPATRICK'S MODEL

Kirkpatrick's model is a four-level planning and evaluation model for training programs. Most instructional designers know about these four levels. What we are going to elucidate here is the new version of the Kirkpatrick's model, which presents the fourth level as the first stage of this planning and evaluation model.

In Kirkpatricks' book (D. and J. Kirkpatrick, 2008), it is cited that the trainers must start by determining the goals and results of the training, then to allocate what behaviors, attitudes, knowledge, and skills are needed to accomplish these results. All this said, it is important though to consider this model as a planning methodology for training rather than evaluation, because applying the four levels after a program was running for some time represents a challenge, if not an impossibility to create a value by applying this model.

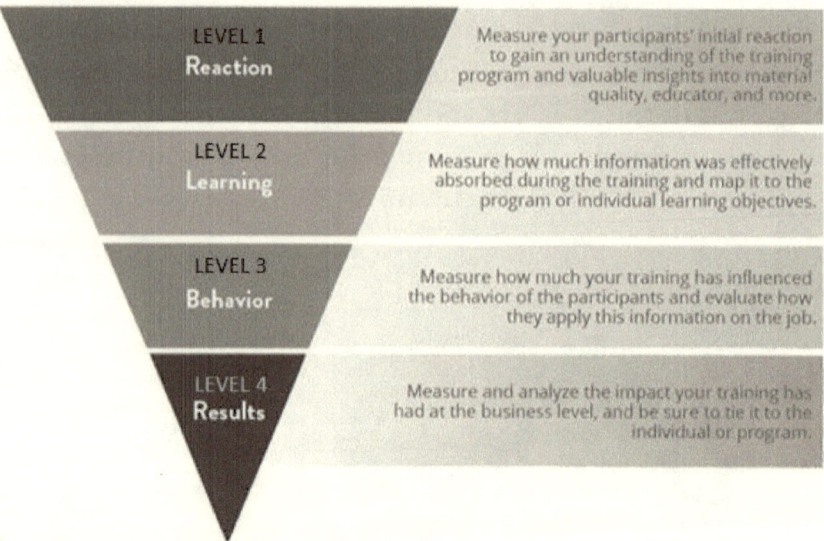

Figure 11. The four levels of Kirkpatrick's model. Available at https://learning.linkedin.com/blog/learning-thought-leadership/ the-best-way-to-use-the-kirkpatrick-model--the-most-common-way-t

Kirkpatrick's model is a process that helps the learning professionals and developers plan and negotiate the expectations of the program before it is set forth. It provides an opportunity to ask questions to clarify the key concepts of the stakeholders to achieve realistic outcomes. Learning professionals will then convert these expectations into observable and measurable outcomes by initiating the planning by asking the question, *What will success look like to you?* The success indicators set by the stakeholders will become the level 4 of the model: the targeted outcomes (J. and W. Kirkpatrick, 2009).

NEEDS ASSESSMENT

Needs assessment (NA) is an evaluation and quality-assurance process that is generated from the analysis phase of instructional design. It is the gap between what an organization expects to have happened and what is actually occurring. Needs assessment allows the designers to understand more about the needs or wants of the client.

To conduct a needs assessment, you need to go through these steps until you can define the gaps and deliver the recommended changes needed for the program, the course or the whole design.

This needs assessment is conducted to improve the design of instruction with mobile considerations for a private school in Dubai during the pandemic situation. These considerations will ideally support the instruction to improve the performance of the students and augment their skills while learning with technology. Therefore, the approach of this needs assessment is a design-based approach (DBR), where we will explore design approaches to enhance the instructional design with mobile learning capabilities.

The school will try to specify the theories of work that will enhance the instruction, describe a workflow that will include steps and strategies to leverage the learning outcome of the students, and incorporate products and solutions from mLearning to get a specific outcome and, thus, come out with an instructional framework needed to implement mobile learning strategies.

To do so, the school decided to conduct a needs assessment to be able to generate a framework that suits their learners and the design of their instruction and curriculum, and then, to identify the needs (gaps) to be readdressed by a strategic framework of instruction and enhance the skills of the students. The mLearning will be measured during the collection of data on two perspectives: *subjective factors* and *objective factors* for learning.

Finally, a report will be delivered to the school administration within three weeks of work as the final framework for mobile learning implementation.

Mobile learning introduced complex design for learning with very few guidelines on how to implement it, that is why it is important to identify, before any implementation, a specific framework to be able to incorporate sound methodology of work that matches the instructional design of the school. And to be able to collect information and build an instructional framework that the school will need, it is important to conduct a needs assessment to study the environment, attitudes, and the engagement of the audience of the school in question, and define the gaps and the needs between the old instruction and the new/desired instruction. This NA will help find the challenges and the gaps to readdress the design by identifying the requirements needed to upgrade the instructional framework with mLearning approaches.

1. Needs Assessment Objectives

The aim of this needs assessment is not only to resize the existing courses of the school eLearning platform only but to optimize the learning outcome using approaches from learning theories and mobile learning–interface capabilities to build a sound framework. Therefore, the objectives of this NA is to find the following needs: Identify the learning capabilities of mLearning, determine the cases for learning that allow mLearning, identify the need for mLearning and the optimization of the learning design, and understand the need to shift the learning approaches for mLearning capabilities and their appropriate use to redesign the instruction.

2. Questions

The questions that the above objectives are imposing for this study are as follows:

- Does the school need to incorporate mLearning?
- What are the approaches that the school will need to incorporate mLearning in their instruction?

- How to optimize eLearning design with mLearning?

3. Methodology

1. *Determine the targeted audience:* This NA is targeting a large audience in the school: K-12 students, teachers, and every educational staff who is interested in participating in the implementation of mLearning. Therefore, the survey conducted was based on qualitative and quantitative questions with students, parents, and academics (teachers, instructional designers from different stages) to collect diverse data (random sampling).

2. *Instruments of the data collection:* The sampling was collected from the most representative persona for the use of mobile learning to get the closest responses to the target audience of the school (K12- students, parents, and academics). Also, the design-based approach of this study requires a meaningful sampling, and as it is mentioned in the literature review (Geuna, 2000, 335), it requires random sampling that we call probability-based design. In addition to that, and in the same reference, it is mentioned that design-based sampling does not require assumptions regarding the population under focus.

However, this type of sampling requires high diversity in the population, which is something available in this school population as it is a private school and the population used has different nationalities, thus the collection of a rich and diverse data is possible. In addition to the particularity of a diverse population as a requirement for the design-based random approach, it is also important to have a high number in the sampling population, and as this was not possible for the limitations of time and number of volunteered people to participate in this survey, the researcher followed mixed sampling approaches to get meaningful data by targeting a small population who can give relatively meaningful information from parents, students, and class teachers.

The survey methods were varying, between qualitative and quantitative data collection.

Quantitative surveys were dispatched from Google Forms, and qualitative interviews were conducted by phone to introduce the concept of conferencing with mobiles. The following questions were asked for the teachers and the instructional designers (educators):

Educators' Qualitative Survey Questions (Descriptive Answers Required)
[1] What are the changes that you can incorporate in your learning method when we will introduce mLearning?
[2] Did you participate in or conducted mLearning designed lessons?
[3] Do you have a particular process to follow or model for mLearning requirements?
[4] What are the technics in teaching that will enable students to perform better when using mLearning in classrooms?
[5] How to upgrade the school eLearning platform with more features that will allow students to have a comfortable mLearning experience at home?

The following sample questions were used for the parents' survey:

Parent's Quantitative Survey Questions	Choice 1	Choice 2	Choice 3
[1] Do you use a mobile, laptop, or tablet to study at home?	Mobile	Laptop/ desktop	Tablet
[2] Which device is more helpful for your child to submit, read, and conduct any activity from school?	Smartphone	Laptop/ desktop	Tablet

[3] How do you find the interface of the school eLearning platform on your personal device?	Easy to use	Confusing	Hard to use
[4] Do you allow your child to work on his personal device in the school?	Yes	No	Maybe.
[5] When do you feel that your child is engaged in his learning?	When using smartphone	When using laptop/ desktop	When using tablet.

The following sample questions were used for the students' survey:

Student's Quantitative Survey Questions	Choice 1	Choice 2	Choice 3
[1] Do you prefer to use hard copy books or soft copy books from the school?	Hard copy	Soft copy	Both
[2] Do you prefer to submit written (with a pen and a paper) assignments scanned and posted or to work on your device directly?	Write with the pen and scanned	Work on my device	No difference for me.
[3] When do you feel that the content of the school is easy to read?	When I work on my mobile.	When I am using my laptop	When I am using my tablet.

[4] Do you think online live sessions are easier when using smartphones?	Yes	No	Maybe
[5] How much time do you spend learning when using your smartphone?	1 to 2 hours	Less than 1 hour	Less time than when using books.

The information collected during the surveys (qualitative and quantitative) helped the researcher understand well the design requirements of mobile learning and how to implement it in the school.

4. Technological Resources

To conduct the present NA, the school used many technologies to collect data. First of all, the administration e-mailed all the school community to inform them about the decision of conducting studies for the possibility of implementing mobile learning as students will be bringing their personal devices to work in the classroom during the pandemic situation, COVID-19, and that no sharing is allowed to prevent the spread of the virus. That is to explain to the school community how the current situation is going to change their learning.

Then, the school started the collection of the data through surveys made on Google Forms to collect quantitative data. More qualitative data was collected from school academics using web conferencing for interviews on smartphones.

Google Classroom for higher grades and Schoology LMS for primary students are other technologies the school used for the delivery of online learning when students were conducting learning from home to test the ability of these platforms to deliver to the school students the right mLearning.

5. Human Resources

The human resources that participated to conduct the following NA are the researcher (me); the teachers, for their knowledge of the levels across the school; the head of the departments, for their input about the assessments and the course contents; SEND teachers, for the requirements and adaptations the school will need to include for SEND students; the IT department, for their input about the technologies used; instructional designers and SMEs across the levels, for their knowledge about the school curriculum and course materials; the school stakeholders, for their input about the funding and material limitations; and the students and the parents were also included in the NA while collecting data for their user experience (UX), which would help in reshaping the school teaching and learning.

6. Process of the Data

The questions designed for the collection of data were divided into subjective and objective factors.

b. *Subjective factors:* Subjective factors are all about learning motivation, learning interest, classroom attraction, persistence, assessment methods, and teaching online and in-classroom practices.

c. *Objective factors:* Objective factors are all about ease of use, platform facilities, features and interfaces, and the way students learn (time and device choices).

Therefore, the findings will be reported according to the above factors.

a. *Objective factors:* Students and parents prefer tablets for reading and assignment work. Smartphones are mostly used by parents to check on their children work, assignments' updates, and school reports only. The LMSs used by the school are both designed to accept mobile and tablet interfaces, which made the percentage of the data in the choice between both learning devices very close. The majority of the participants in the survey agreed on the fact that the online sessions are much easier when using mobile phones or tablets as the quality of the voice is better than using laptops. Instructional designers admitted that they researched the topic of creating an instructional framework based on mobile learning strategies but did not come across good mobile learning that was specific to smartphones only; they all agreed on the fact that the confusion is about the device to use as laptops are considered mobile learning, but in fact, they are not as much portable as smartphones and are not as instantly accessible as laptops, and they have user-support features that keep the device up-to-date.

b. *Subjective factors:* Teachers and educators could not understand the requirements of mobile learning and the capabilities of the mobile device for learning. The school will try to explain the difference in teaching and learning and the capabilities of mobile learning in the redesigning of the educational material. Touchscreen was the only interaction that the academics could include in their course design by using applications that allow students to answer by writing with their fingers or by dragging and dropping the answers. Instructional designers proposed some approaches like the use of *performance support*, which is used for training purposes in the industry field, but the instructional designers proposed to use this approach to facilitate mobile learning a specially for scientific subjects (this point will be elaborated under the below title). Instructional designers and teachers agreed also on the fact that mobile phones are agile devices, but linking the theories of learning with the mobile technologies in constructing a course is not that easy, as it requires features from the device itself and that all they can integrate is collaboration, communication, and diversified activities for their learners, while mobile learning can handle wider opportunities for learning when using learning theories like *enactivism* (this theory will be elaborated below). Some of the feedback came to elaborate on a specific design framework for mobile learning: *Integrative learning design framework*, as a design for the mobile learning integration process. The framework will help redesign the course, as the interviewee said, to create effective interactivity with activities and feedback.

7. Future Actions

According to what was collected from the qualitative and quantitative data, the school decided to create a set of priorities to include in the school curriculum in order to integrate mobile learning properties in the new design framework with the following recommendations:

a. The school recommended that the instructional design should empower self-learning to engage students while using their personal devices and to encourage informal and natural learning by lifting up the limited schedules of assignments and try to integrate learning into their daily-basis activities, like to accommodate short-learning instances that can be visited by the learner on the go.
b. The constructivist approach for learning is also what the school decided to add to the learning design by encouraging authentic activities, forcing the learner to make more researches on the web and come up with a sound answer that is relevant to his specific learning interests.
c. Encourage collaboration and information sharing between the students in a way that makes it a fluent informal chat between them, allowing interaction with one another. The design of the course should not be forcing things to happen,

instead make them look informal, instant, and spontaneous peer-to-peer conversations.

d. Students will need some training, especially for primary school students who need to understand how they effectively collaborate and maintain effective discussions. To do so, the school decided to give more consideration to the performance support instead of training them, which is giving information as a block to the learner. With the performance support, they can receive instant feedback, tips and tricks, and recommendations as short messages while they interact with each other to redirect them to the right use of language or use of the application. The user support system can generate also smileys and icons for the performance of the learner.

e. Situated learning was recommended to be implemented using mobile learning in classrooms especially to record data and observations instantly and information from the classroom, to take pictures from the board for note-taking instead of writing on a notebook. This was not allowed in the school as mobile devices were not allowed inside the classrooms too. The school recommended also to design to this particular feature of the mobile learning specific activities and incorporate the use of the camera in a structured way.

f. New learning theory will be included in the curriculum design, which is the enactivist learning theory (cognitivism blended with constructivism). It is a theory developed by Maurice Merleau-Ponty (Wikipedia, 2018) to explain that learning is not only about one individual, it is also about others in the outer environment, and knowledge is an interaction between the learner, the other learners, and their environment (Sumara and Davis, 1997). It gives an overview on how students learn individually and in groups, explaining that learning should never happen in a classroom only; it has to be informal, too, to reflect the real learning events of the student in new experiences and environments. That is why the school will encourage the use of 3D learning labs and sensor-based games that are embodied in the mobile learning interfaces.

g. The integrative learning design framework (ILDF) is to support learners' literacy with powerful applications to make their reading effective (US National Reading Panel Report 2000). To do so, the school decided to abandon their child-focused literacy program and move to a collaborative story-based program, including computer skills embedded in writing applications.

One of the best practices of blended learning is to redesign the instruction at any occasion or event to include new approaches and create a new framework for learning that suits the school and its audience (McGee and Reis, 2012). This redesigning cannot be done without running a needs assessment evaluation process before the reengineering of the instruction. In this paper, the researcher tried to extract a new framework for the school to redesign the instruction and incorporate new strategies for learning that suited COVID-19 arrangements and blended learning between the classroom and online learning.

Planning and evaluating curriculums and programs is an important step to success. It allows evaluators to analyze and construct their process on concrete information. A good evaluation is measured by comparing the behavior of the learners over time in addition to drawing conclusions about program performance that are justified based on the available evidence. Otherwise, a reevaluation can be processed again and again to align the outcomes to the new challenges that the program can face, as we discussed earlier.

Program planning is a development process that coordinates and facilitates change according to a need or a defined problem. It is a decision-making process where we need to choose the services to achieve impressive outcomes. By planning for our programs, we give a clear insight into the problems to be addressed and provide a continuous program performance assessment.

The planning requires research rather than involving research methods. At the planning, needs assessment is one of the bases of the planning stages where we gather information, data, and prerequisites about our customer or learner, while in the program evaluation, needs assessment provides program evaluators useful information to improve the service delivery and the systems. However, both planning and evaluation must be processed frequently to be able to leverage the level of the training and keep the learning outcomes updated and well-structured with the activities and the tools used.

Chapter VI
PROGRAM DESIGN

In this chapter, we're going to plan for a smart learning ecology: design it and attribute the technology needed for the program, and at the end, evaluate it using the theoretical measures for planning and evaluating programs.

The present design aims to create an online program for an online teaching and learning institution located in UAE, based on digital micro-credentials to help students who are still unfamiliar with eLearning needs and to support them before they get enrolled in their courses' curriculum.

The scope of work is to plan, design, develop, and evaluate a program to assist students who feel at risk of dropping the courses/school or feel unfamiliar with online learning, at the beginning of each semester and/or before they engage in their learning journey at an online institution.

In addition to that, this kind of program is a key for new students who need assistance at the emotional and educational level to be able to engage in their semester with tips, tricks, and useful information about each course they are going to enroll in. Consequently, the online course will enhance their self-confidence, skills, and competencies, and will improve the level of their ability to self-regulate their learning and acknowledge their ability to enroll in more than two courses at once.

The program is going to allow students gain digital badges for each course. Students can gain a certain number of badges, knowing that each badge is measured by learning points. These learning points can be accumulated throughout the semester, and learners will be given a choice to switch their points into a monetary value that they can use for the payment of their school fees. It is also an accumulative system of points that, once it reaches a certain number, it allows its owner to issue badges to other learners for their contribution to their work in a project or in a work review.

This learning system will allow the students to have an idea of what is coming up in their courses, what to expect from the course, what the content (syllabus) is, and the time needed to accomplish the course in a due manner.

At the end of this program, students will gain recognition badges that are authentic, trackable, digitalized, and easy to share on social media or ePortfolio for the betterment of their careers and to showcase their skills. It is in fact a digital artifact that, if well designed, the online institution will be able to standardize their badges according to UAE national standards and introduce these badges as a recognized set of data to represent the achievement associated with a set of skills.

At the end of the journey, each student will collect a set of skills personalized to their learning journey. The present program evaluates students through online self-assessment. It has a set of modules, quizzes, and a self-assessment that will follow the training to measure the learning outcomes according to the standards for eLearning set by MOE.

Program Planning

The overview we will be giving in this section is a short description of what our program will be fixing and what the main learning improvements are that the program will bring to the online institution. It is an introduction to picture all the elements of the program that you will develop later in your design.

The present online program that we're going to name, DARES[1] Program, is designed for an online institution for teaching and learning. It aims to assist students in understanding details related to the courses of the curriculum, the assessments, the modules, the activities, and how much the course can suit their time and personal schedule. It is an invitation to allocate if the course syllabus matches the students' expectations or not, as most of the learners in this online institution are full-time employees.

The program is a confidence booster for the students and is evidence-based learning to reduce the risk of them dropping the courses. In the same time, it teaches students how to become good

---

1   DARES is Arabic, meaning "I studied," "I revised."

researchers with critical thinking and writing skills; it provides digitalized evidence that the students who enrolled and finished the course had gained certain skills and knowledge for their actual school qualification, and for that, they will receive a digital badge that represents the outcome of their learning.

PEDAGOGICAL & PSYCHOLOGICAL LEARNING BASES

Now, it is time to plan your program based on pedagogical approaches and theories you will be using to build your instruction. It is an important step to deploy your techniques of work and to be more persuasive for the stakeholders.

The DARES Program aims to enhance self-regulated learning and increase motivation to help the learner perform better academically.

Cognitive evaluation theory explains the external consequences of internal motivation on students' engagement (Zholdasbekov et al., 2014). In this situation, students are demotivated by the lack of information given by the school to them before enrolling in a course, which makes them uncomfortable with the content during the first two to three weeks of learning. That is why preparing the learning environment with the tools and the assistance they need is important at the beginning of the semester to improve their motivation and self-regulation.

Achievement goal theory focuses on the achievement behavior of the learner and how students evaluate their competences and react as a behavioral result of that. This theory explains how student's comfort at the beginning of the semester can influence their achievement and how they will react accordingly. The behavior of the student can affect the cognitive outcome, which is goal-oriented. If the goal is ambiguous, the student's outcome will be under expectations.

Besides, it is important to take into consideration *self-regulated learning* strategies to involve mental processes and engage the learners through tasks that they can master at the beginning of the semester, which will affect their intrinsic motivation. The DARES Program gives this opportunity to the students and engages them with instant feedback and usage of cognitive and metacognitive strategies, as well as preparing the learner for what it is coming.

At the end of the semester, the digital badge will conclude the DARES Program outcome. It is positive reinforcement for the students that gives them the motive to accomplish more, gain more skills, and go further with the online institution's curriculum by taking the DARES Program as an assistant, a guide, and concrete proof of their academic achievement. This program has a lot of approaches embedded in its course, modules, and assessments; and that we will be highlight below:

Self-learning to promote self-regulated learning is what the online institution needs from its students to achieve their learning with efficacy from the first day of their enrollment to the school. It is known that not all people are self-regulated and find it an easy task for them. The program is meant to conduct self-learning sessions and assessments. However, we are certain that everyone can learn from a video, a storyboarding, or a scenario; and it is an easy task to do, and that is how the present program will present its content to the learners. They will start self-learning to promote self-regulation from the courses given to them under the scope of this program, and they will deepen their skill in self-regulated learning with school courses of their curriculum.

Motivation and positive reinforcement, intrinsic or extrinsic motivation is represented in the badging system because of the attitudes created by them (intrinsic), and the reinforcement theory refined by Skinner has existed for years and is still working with adult learners. Micro-credentials in this program are digital badges, and they represent reinforcements that engage and motivate adult learners to act in certain behaviors to gain the reward associated with them. They are also visual feedback or recognition for their efforts at the end of each course (Ellis et al. 2016).

Outcome-based educational approach (OBE) is to build the program to equip the students with the knowledge they need, the skills and the competencies they lack to engage in a certain activity (Brolin,

1997). This program will equip the students with the skills they need to be successful in their semester and get the best of their learning journey.

THE AUDIENCE AND LEARNER ANALYSIS

Before we design any program or course, we need to conduct a needs assessment as mentioned earlier in chapter 4 during the analysis stage, and the main element we will need is to plan for the success of our program, which is related closely to studying our audience and understanding their needs, wants, values, and beliefs to be able to adjust the program effectively.

The audience intended for this program is graduate or postgraduate students at an online teaching and learning institution. However, the program is not obligatory, and students will have to choose whether they need this program or not, based on their level of self-confidence. No necessary prior knowledge or specific conditions will be required from the student except being a student at the online institution in question, proficient in the language of the program (English per default), and no conditions will be needed to enroll in this program except being new to the online institution and/or feeling anxious about the courses that the curriculum is offering. Students will be free to take this program for their convenience and to decide on the course they think will represent a barrier for them to learning.

The model used to design the instruction of this program is the ADDIE model for instruction. And the first step of the ADDIE model is to conduct learner analysis.

To do so, needs assessment is a must to analyze the program's target audience's needs and wants. It can be applied to measure theses needs and wants of the students and to know their learning styles, prior knowledge, skills, experiences, and job positions. To collect such data, the designer will need to conduct questionnaires, interviews, and checklist-based data collection to identify the following:

- The gaps between student's skills and the skills required to conduct effectively the DARES Program
- Understand the social, technological, and economic situation of the learners and their professions
- Estimate their computer skills and language proficiencies
- The gap between the current and the desired level of the students
- The conditions under which the DARES Program will occur (triangulation)
- To understand what the program topic will include and how and what will be gained from the DARES Program (triangulation)
- Define the goals of the online institution's stakeholders in implementing the DARES Program for their students (triangulation)

Besides, the designer will understand the level of interest and readiness of the students to take this innovative program, how much they know about digital badges, and their attitude for an extra course to take each semester through the attitudinal analysis of the audience (Jurin et al., 2010). It is to address the audience's attitudes, beliefs, values, and what they like and what they dislike.

Once the designer could understand the attitudes of the audience toward the courses and the curriculum, he will redirect his design to the preferences of this audience to be able to give them the right content aligned with the right activity. The designer's question is this: *How do the online institution's students feel toward interactive video courses?*

Beliefs are about what they think is good or bad, true or false. The designer's leading question is this: What do the online institution's students think about being rewarded with an electronic badge?

Values are the standards of the audiences. To understand the values of this institution's students, the designer has to ask, *What are the motives of the students to take this digital extra course?*

To collect attitudinal analysis data, closed-ended questions (yes/no or true/false), multiple-choice questions, and open-ended questions can be sent to the students to understand their attitudes, beliefs, and values toward this program.

COMPARATIVE ANALYSIS

To be able to convince your stakeholders of the importance of your program during the analysis stage of the ADDIE model, it is crucial to compare it to an existing program or to what their organization will look like when they opt for your program. You need to highlight clearly the differences and explain how much they need your program and how much it will enhance the learning experience of their clients. In this section, we will try to explain how much the online institution will need our program and give evidence on the impact of its implementation on their students.

This program is an innovative tool for students to assess their ability to engage in a course with confidence. The online institution does not have such a program implemented and does not use standardized digital badges to deliver against a set of skills. They have local badges that are related to the behavior of the student (perfect attendance, deans' list, etc.). However, these badges are just logos or pictures; they are not digitalized, and they are not shareable on social media nor do they contain information about student's gain of knowledge.

Digital badges in the DARES Program will indicate the trust and quality of the learning and the knowledge provided by the online institution; they are awards for achievement, not for the behavior of the student. They contain detailed information about the skill gained that are verifiable and recognized by the Ministry of Education, with standards for institutional licensure and program accreditation.

Digital badges in this program are innovative tools for the learners. The online institution is used to provide a digital copy of certificates for any students' achievement, but never for the courses they add to their curriculum.

Digital badges can help the learner gather a set of badges that represent only his progress for learning, as each badge represents a course or precisely the skills gained in this course. Students can enroll in a course and top up skills that they are not rewarded for.

With these badges, the ePortfolio of each student will reflect individualized learning skills and competencies. The badges can be shared worldwide through social media and can be added to an ePortfolio or a personal blog of a student. They are pieces of evidence that validate the accomplishment of certain learning stages or courses or gain a set of skills and competencies. Students can add them to their CVs and showcase their work to their employers; they can build up an agenda of their learning journey and the efforts deployed to give more details about the final certificate that they get from their institution by showing what the exact skills gained are, which will give to the learner a better chance in having a job tailored to his competencies and bring in better career opportunities. Badges are not just a picture of a badge; they are identifiable, coded, authentic, and verifiable for reliability.

Program Development

In this section that we will relate to the development stage in the ADDIE model, you will need to list all the resources and tools needed to allocate before and after your program will be running, including human resources (before the implementation stage). It is to give an overview to the stakeholders of the different tools and resources they need to make available for your project.

The school will need to provide human resources and tools to build a high-quality program:

1. *Human Resources.* The school will need to allocate a group of instructional designers and professors specialized in each

curriculum to develop the material and the modules of each program assigned to each department and an IT team for assistance and helpdesk issues.

2. *Tools and Technology.* The program is a technology-based and online-delivered course. The university will need to prepare material that is made by iSpring Suite software. It is a toolkit used to create scenario-based videos for learning. The platform that will log the courses of the DARES Program exists already: it is the same platform of the online institution courses, and the student will find the course that is tailored for him right at the course enrolment dashboard so that he can take the course before he decides on his enrolment. For the rewarding system, the technology used is the digital badges, which has to be standardized and regularized by the Ministry of Education. Usually, and in other schools worldwide, badges are collected through a link sent by the university to the student after achieving the program. The designing software for digital badges can be found online. This will allow the online institution to issue and store digital micro-credentials and open badges. The same website can quickly issue badges to the services or specific people in the organization.

Vision and Mission

Under this title, the designer will need to explain why the program is needed and how it will help the institution, including the problems that the program will fix and the exact skills to gain from it, which is a part of the development stage of the ADDIE model. The designer will also need to highlight the short-term, medium, and long-term goals to prepare for the processing of his logic model.

The vision of this program is to make students confident and self-oriented in deciding on the courses they wish to enroll in before the beginning of the semester. It will reduce students dropping off from courses and prevent loss in time and cost. The program will prepare them emotionally by increasing their knowledge about how much the course will add to their career and their competencies in the field of their curriculum and how to achieve it successfully. It will provide the students with the right skills to become better learners with critical thinking and scientific research skills. The program is based on rewards (digitalized badges) that are easy to share on social media to allow the students to showcase their work and achievement with authentic evidence for their learning.

The goals of this online learning program are clear.

○ *Short-Term Goal.* This is to reduce the risk of dropping from the courses at the online institution by providing the learners the maximum of information they need and assist them with a summarized course syllabus and content before they enroll in the courses at the beginning of each semester.

○ *Medium-Term Goal.* This is to ease the path for the students and enhance their self-confidence, engagement, and motivation in the online institution eLearning curriculum, especially for newly enrolled students and fresh graduates. It gives an overview of the syllabus of the course in question and its requirements: time and delivery schedule, the assignments and their structure, the skills and competencies to gain, and the role of the course in boosting the career of the student.

○ *Long-Term Goal.* The digital badges will follow the goals defined by the relevant course designed for it. If the course has a goal to gain specific skills, then the digital badge will have the same skillset to acquire. Delivering digitalized micro-credentials as a reward is to gain standardized and recognized skillset and develop mastery in key concepts of the course that students can showcase and share in social media.

PROGRAM LOGIC MODEL

INPUTS	ACTIVITIES	OUTPUTS	OUTCOMES
HUMAN RESOURCES	Lectures, quizzes, storyboards, and self-assessments. The activities are presented in interactive videos through modules.	Students will inspect, identify, and practice the course syllabus, activities and all related prerequisites to be able to enroll in the course with necessary background knowledge and skills.	**SHORT-TERM**
instructional designers, professors specialized for each curriculum, IT and helpdesk employees, technicians for creating materials.			Students' readiness for the course; Become comfortable with the course syllabus, material, and assignments; Have enough information about the requirements of the course: time and delivery schedule;
TOOLS & TECHS	**PARTICIPANTS**		**MEDIUM-TERM**
Graphic computers High definition and performance for graphics, software and websites.	• Students at the Online Institute in question. • Course Facilitators. • IT help-desk.		Reduce drop-off from courses in the middle of the semester; Gain micro-credentials for the skills learned and being eligible for digital badges at the achievement of the course. Develop mastery in key concepts of the course.
			LONG-TERM
			Career booster. Gain standardized and recognized skillset easy to share on social media.

PROGRAM LEARNING OUTCOMES

Then the designer will write the program learning outcomes (PLO) in detail according to *what*, *how well*, *how*, and *when* these learning outcomes are going to be measured in our course. At the end of this section, the designer will write the overall learning outcome statement of his learning design.

The main goal of the DARES Program is that students will be effective self-regulated learners with critical thinking skills in courses of their curriculum and highly motivated for the enrollment. The following guidelines are adapted from Tom Angelo's workshop (2013) to the program requirements:

- *What* students will be able to organize and deliver analytical and creative writing for the courses of their curriculum.
- *How Well* (expectations) students will become self-regulated learners with research and writing skills in their domain.
- *How* (which material): interactive video courses.
- *When*: At the end of the semester.

The following table is an overview of how the instructional designer should organize his PLO to include all the above information in detail and finally end the PLO with the statement as shown in this section.

PROGRAM LEARNING OUTCOMES			
GOALS What students will be	**WHAT** Students will be able to	**HOW WELL** Expectations	**WHEN** When it should be completed by
Define the syllabus purpose and main content of the course in question.	Identify the schedule, type of assignments, quizzes and tests, tasks, and the delivery mode required by the course and textbook required.	Demonstrate the ability to solve similar tasks, quizzes, and assignments with high performance (critical thinking and creativity).	At the beginning of the course.
Recall prior knowledge and link it to the content structure.	Construct new knowledge about the course content, theories, approaches, and models.	Integrate prior knowledge with the new knowledge to build new skills and competencies.	In the middle of the course.
Demonstrate learning of theories and skills relevant to this course that provide the foundation for building an impactful practice.	Recognize the most cited theorists, mode of work, approaches, and new practices and challenges.	Employ theories, models, and methods of this context in a meaningful way.	At the end of the course.

Support arguments and analyze scenarios with specific consideration to the theories and approaches studied to demonstrate the gain of new skills and competencies.	Justify their answers using theories, approaches, and models related to the course content.	Cite their work using theorists' names and books the most relevant to the content to demonstrate synthesis and critical thinking skills.	At the assessment stage.

Now, let's write the final statement of the DARES Program Learning Outcomes:

"At the end of this program, students of the online institution will be effective self-regulated learners with critical thinking skills and highly motivated for enrollment. They will be able to organize and deliver analytical with critical thinking skills in writing about topics of their curriculum and meet syllabus expectations for each criterion with the interactive video courses."

IMPLEMENTATION STRATEGIES

The program we're working on should be clearly described, including its implementation strategies. It will help the stakeholder understand its requirements and cope with the budgeting of the program. While describing the program features, it will be wise to give examples to explain the point of view of the designer, especially when the program is bringing up big changes at the host institution.

This program is an online-based course. The students will have for each course modules to accomplish with a quiz at the end of each module (formative assessment) and a final self-assessment at the end of the program (summative assessment). The student will choose to take the course, or not, and start learning through a set of videos.

Then, he will have to conduct a quiz at the end of each module and answer some questions about what was explained in the videos. At the end of the course's program, the student will have to go through an assessment to show their understanding of the content and their ability to enroll in the relevant course without hesitation. Once the learner has successfully passed the final exam of the course of the online institution curriculum, an e-mail will be sent automatically to his inbox to collect his badge for the course through a link. Let's give an example on that:

Let's say that a given student has to enroll in a course called SAB-622, and before he enrolls, he needed more information about the course syllabus, the schedule, the content of the modules, and his ability to pass the final exam with a high score. He needs to know also if the workload is suitable for his own work schedule and family duties or not. So he decided to take the DARES Program (it is just forty-five minutes). He takes the program, understands that SAB-622 is a good course for his skillset and professional development, but it has a lot of assignments and tasks, which does not match his daily responsibilities, so he decides not to enroll in this course, especially that he just relocated and moved to another city.

COURSE AND MODULE STRUCTURE

In this study plan, the designer will try to explicit how the course modules are going to be conducted as a part of his implementation stage for the application of the ADDIE model, by giving more details for each module structure and incorporating the tools and resources needed to accomplish the course program and the schedule of its module.

The duration of one course is set at forty-five minutes. Each session (module) will last for ten minutes, plus fifteen minutes of self-assessment. The course snapshot will demonstrate the duration of the modules and what the learner will know in each module.

The following program study plan is made for the course modules that are shown in the course snapshot, designed to include the objectives, resources, content of the modules, and the time spent on each module.

The content of the study plan was adapted from a template found at PRAXIS ETS. Modules 1, 2, 3, and the self-assessment will be displayed to the student each in a separate video located at the dashboard of the DARES Program. The student will have three interactive videos of ten minutes each, including quizzes, and one interactive video of fifteen minutes for a self-assessment session. The interactive videos will include websites and readings that will be considered extra material for the student to deepen their knowledge of the topic. Each module will be structured as follows:

COURSE SNAPSHOP FOR DARES PROGRAM
MODULE 1 . . . . 10 mins
Introduction to the course | *Interactive video + quiz*
Syllabus required by the course in question
(textbook, delivery method of the course, time & holidays scheduled, assignments and quizzes)
MODULE 2 . . . . 10 mins
Information about the Modules of the course | *Interactive video + quiz*
Course assignments and modules
(Prior knowledge, new knowledge, theories, approaches & models)
MODULE 3 . . . . 10 mins
Main content of the course to take | *Interactive video + quiz*
Modules Content summary
(Most cited theorists in the field, new practices and challenges)
SELF-ASSESSMENT . . . . 15 mins
Interactive video
(Justify answers using theories, creatively relate the approaches and models studied to a self-experience)

Module 1	
Content Covered	Course Syllabus **Introduction & Overview**
Description of the Content	Identify the main textbook, areas of study, delivery method of the course, and time scheduled throughout the year including holidays and celebrations, assignments and quizzes including special requirements made by the course lecturer.
How Well (Scale from 1–5)	2
What Resources Need to Use?	The interactive video of the program. Course Syllabus & main Textbook (of the course in question).
Where to Find the Resources	Online Institution Home dashboard; DARES Program. Course Syllabus and resources.
Study Schedule	At the beginning of the semester, before enrollment to the course in question.
Study Time	10 minutes

Module 2	
Content Covered	Course Syllabus **Modules Content Summary**
Description of the Content	Recall prior knowledge and link it to the new course content, theories, approaches, models.
How Well (Scale from 1–5)	2
What Resources Need to Use?	The interactive video of the program with links embedded for extra content. Textbook (of the course in question).

Where to Find the Resources	Online Institution Main dashboard; DARES Program application. Course Syllabus
Study Schedule	At the beginning of the semester, before enrollment to the course in question. The first sequence of the module.
Study Time	10 minutes

	Module 3
Content Covered	Course Syllabus **Content Storyboard**
Description of the Content	Recognize the most cited theorists in the field, mode of work, new practices, and challenges.
How Well (Scale from 1–5)	3
What Resources Need to Use?	The interactive video of the program with links embedded for extra content. Textbook (of the course in question). Recommended references (summarized)
Where to Find the Resources	Online Institution Main dashboard; DARES Program application. Course Syllabus
Study Schedule	At the beginning of the semester, before enrollment to the course in question. The second sequence of the module.
Study Time	10 minutes

	QUIZ
Content Covered	Evaluation of **Formative Assessment**
Description of the Content	Determine whether an idea, reference or information has the correct argument or not.

How Well (Scale from 1–5)	4
What Resources Need to Use?	The interactive video of the program with links embedded for extra content. Textbook (of the course in question). Recommended references (summarized)
Where to Find the Resources	Online Institution Main dashboard; Dares Program application. Course Syllabus
Study Schedule	At the beginning of the semester, before enrollment to the course in question. The last sequence of the module.
Study Time	3-4 minutes incorporated in each module

	Self-assessment
Content Covered	Evaluation of **Summative Assessment**
Description of the Content	Support arguments and analyze scenarios with specific consideration to the theories and approaches to demonstrate the skills gained.
How Well (Scale from 1–5)	5
What Resources Need to Use?	The interactive video of the program with links embedded for extra content. Textbook (of the course in question). Recommended references (summarized)
Where to Find the Resources	Online Institution Main dashboard; Dares Dares Program application. Course dashboard; Syllabus
Study Schedule	At the beginning of the semester, before enrollment to the course in question. Self-assessment session.
Study Time	15 minutes

PROGRAM FEATURES

In the implementation stage, the designer will need to give more details on the tools, technologies, and requirements needed to conduct the courses of the program and what will happen when the student accomplishes his course. The rewarding for the program accomplishment must be mentioned as well.

Learning Tools: Interactive videos with storyboarding (built-in quizzes) are the main learning tools of this online program. Interactive means that the video can have elements to drag and drop, to cross, to tick, and to match to make it inclusive of quizzes and to engage the learner in an interactive and engaging session.

The authoring tool that we can use for such type of videos is called iSpring Suit. It is a PowerPoint-based software that needs no training or professional user to build a course based on storyboards and can provide the adequate interactive video-based eLearning for this program. Online institution learner's platform (LMS) is a required tool to lodge the DARES Program.

Social Interaction: The DARES Program will require an individual effort to deploy. No sharing or social interaction will be afforded to conduct the modules or the final self-assessment session. However, after completing the course, and at the end of the semester, social interaction will be gained through the digital badges earned. Students can then share their micro-credentials on social media, showcase their skills on their ePortfolios, and add them to their CVs for career-boosting.

The future of the digital badges is to collect several points that allow students to issue badges to other learners who contributed positively to their learning via writing a project or reviewing an article or even for valuable peer feedback. Badges can be used as a learning recognition system to identify a set of skills achieved. This set is very personalized to the learner's experiences and skills, which can be tracked in a digital environment especially if the badges are standardized.

Learning Technologies: Now, enrolling in this program is elective and depends on the necessity of each student. Does this make it unrequested? The answer is in the reward that the student can get from this program. The course for which the student will choose to take its training will be rewarded for it at the end of the semester by a digital badge. The digital micro-credential is a competency-based rewarding system where the skills gained will be visible and easy to add to ePortfolios and CVs.

The badge is not just a picture, but it has an anatomy:

-   The badge name will include the name of the course in question;
-   the URL is the link that will lead to the collection of the badge with a detailed description of the skills gained; the criteria will include the requirements that a badge earner had to meet in order to earn a given badge; the image is the badge design that is displayed; the issuer is the institution or the establishment, in this case, the online institution; issue date of the badge; the recipient of the badge; the tags describe the badge's topics, competencies, or type of achievement; the alignment of the standards (following international or national standards); the expiration date of the badge, and the URL link of the evidence (authentication of the badge).

EFFECTIVENESS OF THE ASSESSMENTS

In this section, we're going to relate the assessments of the program with the outcomes of the program to evaluate the effectiveness of the assessments designed for the program as part of the evaluation stage of the ADDIE model. In the following, you will find how to align the goals set for the program with the assessments to take.

Critical Thinking and Problem Solving: The DARES Program is set to teach students how to think critically, how to analyze situations using what they learned, and activate their thinking to leverage their level at a researcher's rank. It is a type of program that changes the learner's behavior by showing them where to find the right information, how to analyze the content based on literature, and what to learn to be able to achieve that purpose. In addition to that, problem-solving skills are also one of the bones of this learning program.

It conducts quizzes that propose situations from the real world and gives to the learner the opportunity to conduct a metacognitive learning process by communicating the problem and the issues (storyboarding) that can be faced, then lets the student gather information from the course content to be able to solve problems properly and generate solutions, then evaluate the outcomes at the end of the program by a self-assessment session. If the student finds out that his learning was not achieved properly, he can retake the modules for a second time until he is satisfied by his learning outcome.

Self-Assessment and Its Alignment with PLO: Self-assessment must reflect how much the objectives of the program are met and aligned with the instructional strategies. To be able to align objectives, instructional strategies, and self-assessment, I built up rubrics to measure the progress of the students.

- o For the formative assessment (quizzes), instant feedback is what keeps the student's engagement and motivation in its higher levels and keeps them on track so that before they move to the next module, they already know their weaknesses and strengths, what they have to learn again, and what they already assimilated.
- o For the summative assessment (self-assessment), the criteria being measured must be clearly stated in the rubrics (or checklist if used instead) to measure the intended outcome (Gaytan, 2002). The main purpose of assessments is to monitor student learning, enhance the program, and challenge the students to think further about the content. In addition to that, it is to give better solutions with what they learned to foster a student-centered learning environment and measure learning outcomes. Self-assessment in the DARES Program is standing for what we call in literature self-test.

It is an effective tool to provide immediate feedback related to their achievement before they enroll in the school courses and get exams and assignments. Self-tests prepare the students for the main exams. The DARES Program allows the students to repass the self-assessment before the final exam of the school course as a revision to the content taught. To measure the outcomes of the DARES self-assessment, rubrics are developed for each course assessment to measure what needs to be known, the usage of critical thinking, and the level of analytical thinking using strategies, references, theories, approaches, and models to justify their answers and to showcase their critical thinking skills and their ability to conduct high-quality researches.

The following is a type of rubrics the DARES Program can use to measure the outcomes of the course. The rubrics were based on the general objectives and outcomes of the program: critical thinking, quality content writing, analytical skills, and ability to research using references and citations in a certain topic. The rubrics were automatically generated by a free online software based on the criteria inserted.

DARES Program Self-assessment

Name: _____

	4. Distinguished	3. Proficient	2. Apprentice	1. Novice
Research-Documentation: Bibliography and citation	Project bibliography or credits were complete and flawlessly formatted. All sources were cited and media included captions showing source.	Project bibliography or credits were complete. All information and media sources were cited.	Project bibliography or credits were incomplete. Less than half of the sources were cited.	Did not include project bibliography or credits. One or two sources were cited.
Content-Quality of Information: Relates to topic, detailed, and accurate	All information was clear and came from reputable sources. Extensive details and relevant examples were used to support the content.	Used relevant information. Included many details and strong examples that came from reputable sources.	Information related to the topic, but project needed more details and examples to fully support ideas.	Information did not include details or examples that related to the topic. Information did not come from a reliable source.
Design-Creativity and Originality: Creative design and original artwork	Design was unique and interesting. Used more than five original media items.	Design was original. Used three to five original media items.	Made a few changes to background or layout. Used one or two original media items.	Used only design templates. Media and ideas were not original.
Writing-Ideas: Interesting, informative details	All details were unique, interesting, and related to and supported the main idea. Writing included information based on personal experience.	Writing had many interesting details which supported the main idea. Writing included information based on personal experience.	Writing had three or more details that supported the main idea.	Writing had few details.
Planning-Research and Notes: Quality and quantity	Used six or more reliable sources of information. Notes are clear, organized, and complete.	Used four or five sources of information. No more than one source of information was not reliable. Notes were organized and complete.	Used two or three sources of information. Some of the sources were not reliable. Notes were not complete.	Used only one source of information, or did not use a reliable source. Notes were not clear or missing.

Figure 12. Rubrics of the DARES Program self-assessment.

PROGRAM EVALUATION

When we plan our program, it is also necessary to identify the approaches needed for evaluation purposes and the instruments that will be used before, during, and after the implementation of the program to measure the alignment of its outcomes with the goals set by the stakeholders and the educational team. To do so, the designer will propose a set of evaluation approaches and instruments and highlight the purpose of each evaluation. The following is an example of what the DARES Program will require for its evaluation.

There are five evaluation approaches. We will use all except managing evaluation. This latter is a type of tool we need when we ask for an external agency to undertake the evaluation of the program. In this case of program designing, we will conduct the evaluation study in-house.

A meta-model framework for evaluating the program consists of five evaluation forms where we will discuss the *why* of the evaluation to explain the purpose of using these approaches (Owen, 2007).

Proactive Evaluation: This evaluation takes place before the designing phase of the program. It is to understand what type of program is needed or what format is required. It will help the designer of the program understand why we're going to need this program and what the gap is that we're going to address with this implementation. It will also help us know how we're going to implement it with the best practices possible. At this level, the designer will create the benchmarks to be used in the implementation of the program processes to have effective outcomes. The designer will need to make a research synthesis to find other applications of the same program and to have background knowledge about the problems to be addressed and how to bridge the gap between the research and the real application. To do so, the designer will need to make a needs assessment to understand what the audience's needs and wants are in the online institution community of learners.

Clarificative Evaluation: This evaluation is applied during the development stage of the program, and the designer will try to understand what the outcomes of this program are and how to design to get these outcomes. It is also to understand what the program structures and aspects are that will help in shaping the outcomes and if the program looks reasonable to be applied. At this evaluation, we will build a logic model to understand the relationship between the inputs and the outcomes and the assumptions and objectives. It is, in fact, a clear representation as shown above in this program design. At the end, the designer or the evaluator will gather the needed information and evidence that explains why or why not the program will be successfully implemented.

Interactive Evaluation: It is made to improve the program with ongoing service and structural arrangements while stressing on the process of the program implementation. To be able to find the gaps, the designer needs to ask himself, What is this program trying to achieve? Is it delivering the course that is intended to be delivered? If no, how to address the gaps so that the delivery becomes more effective? The developmental evaluation is an approach that involves many parties and program developers on an ongoing improvement process, especially when the program is standing as a new program or innovative like this program.

Monitoring Evaluation: It is an evaluation form that goes with programs that are established and running for some time. It is used to gather evidence and indication that the program is successful for the stakeholders or the managers to explain the funding of the program. It is usually a quantitative indicator for performance, and it is a regular task to control the progress of the program. The questions that the evaluator will ask are these: Did the program reach the targeted audience? How is the progression of the program now compared to a year ago? How to make the program more effective? The approach needed for the evaluation of this program is the component analysis. It is to evaluate a component in a program, identified as problematic because of the gathered evidence. And that is the component that needs to be reviewed.

Impact Evaluation: It is used to evaluate the effects of the program after a given time of running, such as a mid-term review, or to decide whether it is possible to be implemented in another institution or not. The typical questions to ask for this form are these: What are the unplanned outcomes for this program? Does another type of implementation of the same program have an impact on the outcomes? Is it a cost-effective program? The approach for this form is a process-outcome evaluation study. It measures the outcomes and also the degree of the implementation.

It helps also in processing a summative evaluation role, and in our program, it is important to measure the impact of the program on the other courses of the curriculum.

REFERENCES

Abdullah, M. R. T. L., & Siraj, S. (2010). M-learning curriculum design for secondary school: A needs analysis. *World Academy of Science, Engineering and Technology, 42*, 1624–1629.

Aguilar, O. M., & Krasny, M. E. (2011). Using the communities of practice framework to examine an after-school environmental education program for Hispanic youth. *Environmental Education Research, 17*(2), 217–233. https://doi.org/10.1080/13504622.2010.531248

Angelo, T. (2013). Crafting Clearer Student Learning Outcomes for Better-Aligned Courses and Programs: *The 2013 Assessment Institute in Indianapolis.* Materials for Workshop Session 12K.

Annals of the University Dunarea de Jos of Galati: Fascicle: I, Economics & Applied Informatics. (2017). *Vol. 23* Issue 1, pp. 21–30, 10.

Artino, A. R. J. (2008). Cognitive load theory and the role of learner experience: An abbreviated review for educational practitioners. *Association for the Advancement of Computing In Education Journal (AACE) Journal, 16*, 425–439. Retrieved from http://www.editlib.org/p/25229

Assessing student performance: exploring the purpose and limits of testing. (1994). *Choice Reviews Online, 31*(10), 31-5581-31–5581. https://doi.org/10.5860/choice.31-5581

Athreya, B. H., Mouza, C., Athreya, B. H., & Mouza, C. (2017). Strategies and Tools for Learning to Think. In *Thinking Skills for the Digital Generation* (pp. 123–144). Springer International Publishing. https://doi.org/10.1007/978-3-319-12364-6_8

Ausubel, D. P. (1960). The use of advance organizers in the learning and retention of meaningful verbal material. *Journal of Educational Psychology, 51*(5), 267–272. https://doi.org/10.1037/h0046669

Ausubel, D. P., Novak, J. D., & Hanesian, H. (1978). *Educational psychology: A cognitive view*. New York: Holt, Rinehart and Winston.

Azmi, F. T. (2008). Mapping the learn-unlearn-relearn model: Imperatives for strategic management. *European Business Review, 20*(3), 240–259. https://doi.org/10.1108/09555340810871437

Bandura, A. (1977). *Social Learning Theory*. Englewood Cliffs: Prentice-Hall.

Bandura, A. (1986). Social foundations of thought and action: a social cognitive theory/Albert Bandura. *New Jersey: Prentice-Hall, 1986, 16*(1), 2–xiii, 617.

Bannan-Ritland, B. (2003). The Role of Design in Research: The Integrative Learning Design Framework. *Educational Researcher, 32*(1), 21–24. https://doi.org/10.3102/0013189X032001021

Barab, S. A., & Duffy, T. (2000). From practice fields to communities of practice. *Theoretical Foundations of Learning Environments, 1*, 25–55. Beard, C., and Wilson, J. P. (2013) Experiential

Learning: A Handbook for Education, Training and Coaching (Vol. 3ʳᵈ ed.). London: Kogan Page.

Berking, P., Birtwhistle, M., and Haag, J. (2013). MoTIF Project Mobile Learning Survey Report. Retrieved from http://motif.adlnet.gov

Black, J. B., & McClintock, R. O. (1995). An interpretation construction approach to constructivist design. *Constructivist Learning Environments: Case Studies in Instructional Design*, 25–31. Retrieved from http://books.google.com/books?hl=en&lr=&id=mpsHa5f712wC&oi=fnd&pg=PA25&dq=An+Interpretation+Construction+Approach+to+Constructivist+Design&ots=sXakDjd-Pj&sig=1-Ewda-DZHM0wALZtMI1YXXB76Q

Borders, M. (2019, 1 1). Artificial Intelligence vs. Collective Intelligence. Social Evolution.

Brolin, D. E. (1997). Life Centered Career Education: A Competency-Based Approach.

Brooks, D. C., McCormack, M., & Shulman, B. (2019). Higher Education's 2019 Trend Watch & Top 10 Strategic Technologies. *Educause*, *1*(1), 45. Retrieved from https://library.educause.edu/resources/2020/1/higher-educations-2020-trend-watch-and-top-10-strategic-technologiesEdgar, D. W. (2012). Learning theories and historical events affecting instructional design in education: Recitation literacy toward extraction literacy practices. *SAGE Open*, *2*(4), 1–9. https://doi.org/10.1177/2158244012462707

Brown, J. S., Gray, E. S., Seely Brown, J., & Solomon Gray, E. (1995). The People Are the Company. *Fast Company*, *1*(1), 78–82. Retrieved from http://www.fastcompany.com/26238/people-are-company

Buller, J. L. (2015). *Change Leadership in Higher Education: A Practical Guide to Academic Transformation.* (pp. 1–264). Wiley. https://doi.org/10.1002/9781119210825

Burnes, B. (2020). The Origins of Lewin's Three-Step Model of Change. *Journal of Applied Behavioral Science, 56*(1), 32–59. https://doi.org/10.1177/0021886319892685.

Butler, D. L. (1998). A strategic content learning approach to promoting self-regulated learning by students with learning disabilities. In D. H. Schunk & B. J. Zimmerman (Eds.), *Self-regulated learning: From teaching to self-reflective practice.* (pp. 160–183). New York, NY US: Guilford Publications. Retrieved from http://search.ebscohost.com/login.aspx?direct=true&db=psyh&AN=1998-07519-008&lang=ja&site=ehost-live

Channon, D. F., & Caldart, A. A. (2015). McKinsey 7S model. In *Wiley Encyclopedia of Management* (pp. 1–1). John Wiley & Sons, Ltd. https://doi.org/10.1002/9781118785317.weom120005

Chant, R. H., Moes, R., & Ross, M. (2009). Curriculum Construction and Teacher Empowerment: Supporting Invitational Education with a Creative Problem Solving Model. *Journal of Invitational Theory & Practice, 15*, 55–67. Retrieved from https://login.e.bibl.liu.se/login?url=https://search.ebscohost.com/login.aspx?direct=true&db=aph&AN=48480769&site=eds-live&scope=site

Checkland, P., & Poulter, J. (2006). *Learning for action. J. Wiley & Sons.* (p. 184). London, John Wiley & Sons.

Cheng, Z. and Newby, T. (2019). Instructional Digital Badges: Effective Learning Tools. Educational Technology Research and Development. 10.1007/s11423-019-09719-7.

Chiu, C. M., Hsu, M. H., & Wang, E. T. G. (2006). Understanding knowledge sharing in virtual communities: An integration of social capital and social cognitive theories. *Decision Support Systems, 42*(3), 1872–1888. https://doi.org/10.1016/j.dss.2006.04.001.

Christie, M., Carey, M., Robertson, A., & Grainger, P. (2015). Putting transformative learning theory into practice. *Australian Journal of Adult Learning, 55*(1), 9–30.

Collins, A., Seeley Brown, J., and Holum, A. (1991). *Cognitive Apprenticeship: Making Thinking Visible*. American Educator, 15(3), 6–11, 38–46. Retrieved from https://learningenvironmentsdesign.pressbooks.com/chapter/collin-brown-holum-cognitive-apprenticeship-making-thinking-visible/

Conole, G., & Wills, S. (2013). Representing learning designs - making design explicit and shareable. *Educational Media International, 50*(1), 24–38. https://doi.org/10.1080/09523987.2013.777184

Daniel, J. (2012). Making Sense of MOOCs: Musings in a Maze of Myth, Paradox and Possibility. *Journal of Interactive Media in Education, 2012*(3), 18. https://doi.org/10.5334/2012-18

Daniels, S. R., Wang, G., Lawong, D., & Ferris, G. R. (2017). Collective assessment of the human resources management field: Meta-analytic needs and theory development prospects for the future. *Human Resource Management Review, 27*(1), 8–25. https://doi.org/10.1016/j.hrmr.2016.09.002

DeMartino, D.J. (1999). Employing Adult Education Principles in Instructional Design. In J. Price, J. Willis, D. Willis, M. Jost & S. Boger-Mehall (Eds.), *Proceedings of SITE 1999—Society for Information Technology & Teacher Education International Conference* (pp. 783-788). Waynesville, NC USA: Association for the Advancement of Computing in Education (AACE).

Retrieved December 22, 2020 from https://www.learntechlib.org/primary/p/7838/

Dewey, J. (1916). The democratic conception of education. *Democracy and Education: An Introduction to the Philosophy of Education.*

Diamond R.M. (2013). *Designing and Assessing Courses and Curricula: A Practical Guide*, 3rd Edition.

Diamond, J., & Gonzalez, P. C. (2014). Digital badges for teacher mastery: an exploratory study of a competency-based professional development badge system. *CCT Reports, Center for Children and Technology*, (November), 1–64.

Dunlop, L., Clarke, L., & McKelvey-Martin, V. (2019). Free-choice learning in school science: a model for collaboration between formal and informal science educators. *International Journal of Science Education, Part B: Communication and Public Engagement*, 9(1), 13–28. https://doi.org/10.1080/21548455.2018.1534023

Ellis, L. E., Nunn, S. G., and Avella, J. T. (2016). Digital badges and micro-credentials: Historical overview, motivational aspects, issues, and challenges. In *Foundation of Digital Badges and Micro-Credentials: Demonstrating and Recognizing Knowledge and Competencies* (pp. 3–21). Springer International Publishing. https://doi.org/10.1007/978-3-319-15425-1_1

Estellés-Arolas, E. (2018). The need of Co-utility for successful crowdsourcing. In *Studies in Systems, Decision and Control* (Vol. 110, pp. 189–200). Springer International Publishing. https://doi.org/10.1007/978-3-319-60234-9_11

Faraj, S., Jarvenpaa, S. L., & Majchrzak, A. (2011). Knowledge collaboration in online communities. *Organization Science*, 22(5), 1224–1239. https://doi.org/10.1287/orsc.1100.0614.

Frisendal, T. (2012). BUSINESS CONCEPT MAPPING. In *the Fifth Int. Conference on Concept Mapping*. Valletta, Malta. Retrieved from http://cmc.ihmc.us/cmc2012papers/cmc2012-p23.pdf

Gagné, R. M., & Merrill, M. D. (1990). Integrative goals for instructional design. *Educational Technology Research and Development, 38*(1), 23–30. https://doi.org/10.1007/BF02298245

Galanis, N., Mayol, E., Alier, M., & García-Peñalvo, F. J. (2016). Supporting, evaluating and validating informal learning. A social approach. *Computers in Human Behavior, 55*, 596–603. https://doi.org/10.1016/j.chb.2015.08.005

Gallagher, S. (2018). Educating the right stuff: Lessons in enactivist learning. *Educational Theory, 68*(6), 625–641. https://doi.org/10.1111/edth.12337.

Garaus, C., Furtmuller, G., & Güttel, W. H. (2016, March 1). The hidden power of small rewards: The effects of insufficient external rewards on autonomous motivation to learn. *Academy of Management Learning and Education*. George Washington University. https://doi.org/10.5465/amle.2012.0284

Gary R. M., Steven M. R., Howard K. K., Jerrold E. K. (2012). *Designing Effective Instruction, 7ʰ Edition*.

Gaytan, J., and McEwen, B. C. (2007). Effective online instructional and assessment strategies. *International Journal of Phytoremediation, 21*(1), 117–132.

Geuna, S. (2000, November 20). Appreciating the difference between design-based and model-based sampling strategies in quantitative morphology of the nervous system. *Journal of Comparative Neurology*. https://doi.org/10.1002/1096-9861(20001120)427:3<333::AID-CNE1>3.0.CO;2-T

Harasim, L. (2017). *Learning Theory and Online Technologies*. 1–60, New York.

Hazenburg, C. (2020). Flipped Learning Maximises in-class engagement. *GESS Conference*, Dubai, UAE.

Hox, J. J. (2010). *Multilevel analysis: Techniques and applications: Second edition. Multilevel Analysis: Techniques and Applications: Second Edition* (pp. 1–382). Routledge Taylor & Francis Group. https://doi.org/10.4324/9780203852279

Hrivnak, G. A. (2011). Designing and Assessing Courses and Curricula: A Practical Guide. *Academy of Management Learning & Education, 9*(2), 358–360. https://doi.org/10.5465/amle.2010.51428562

Jezegou, A. (2013). The Influence of the Openness of an E-Learning Situation on Adult Students' Self-Regulation. *International Review of Research In Open And Distance Learning, 14*(3), 182–201.

Jirgensons, M., & Kapenieks, J. (2018). Blockchain and the Future of Digital Learning Credential Assessment and Management. *Journal of Teacher Education for Sustainability, 20*(1), 145–156. https://doi.org/10.2478/jtes-2018-0009.

Johassen, D. H. (1991). Evaluating constructivist learning. *Educational Technology, 31*(9), 28–33.

Jonassen, D. H. (1998). *Task Analysis Methods for Instructional Design. Task Analysis Methods for Instructional Design*. Routledge. https://doi.org/10.4324/9781410602657

Jonassen, D. H., & Rohrer-Murphy, L. (1999). Activity theory as a framework for designing constructivist learning environments. *Educational Technology Research and Development, 47*(1), 61–79. https://doi.org/10.1007/BF02299477

Jurin, R. R., Roush, D., Danter, K. J., Jurin, R. R., Roush, D., & Danter, J. (2010). Analyzing Your Audience. In *Environmental Communication. Second Edition* (pp. 83–105). Springer Netherlands. https://doi.org/10.1007/978-90-481-3987-3_6

Kearsley, G., & Knowles, M. (2010). Andragogy—the theory into practice database. *Retrieved October.*

Kenny, R., Zhang, Z., Schwier, R., & Campbell, K. (2005). A Review of What Instructional Designers Do: Questions Answered and Questions Not Asked. *Canadian Journal of Learning and Technology / La Revue Canadienne de l'apprentissage et de La Technologie, 31*(1). https://doi.org/10.21432/t2jw2p

Kim, T., Cho, J. Y., & Lee, B. G. (2013). Evolution to Smart Learning in public education: A case study of Korean public education. In *IFIP Advances in Information and Communication Technology* (Vol. 395, pp. 170–178). https://doi.org/10.1007/978-3-642-37285-8_18

Kirkpatrick, D. L., & Kirkpatrick, J. D. (2008). *Evaluating Training Programs: The Four Levels. Evaluating Training Programs* (pp. 3–15). San Francisco, CA: Berrett-Koehler Publishers.

Kirkpatrick, D. L., & Kirkpatrick, J. D. (2009). Evaluating: part of a ten-step process. *Evaluating Training Programs,* 3–20.

Knowles, M. S. (1970). The Modern Practice of Adult Education: Andragogy versus pedagogy. *Cambridge Adult Education,* 384.

Knowles, M. S. (1975). Self-directed learning: a guide for learners and teachers. *Selfdirected Learning A Guide for Learners and Teachers.* Philadelphia, Pennsylvania: Cambridge Adult Education, 1975.

Knowles, M. S. (1980). The Modern Practice of Adult Education. *Business*, 400. Retrieved from http://www.amazon.co.uk/dp/0695814729

Lee, J. Zo, H. Lee, H. (2014). Smart learning adoption in employees and HRD managers. *Br. J. Educ. Technol.* *45*(6), 1082–1096.

Lewin, K. (1951). *Field theory in social science: selected theoretical papers (Edited by Dorwin Cartwright). Harpers* (p. 346 pp.).

Lu, J., and Law, N. (2012). Online peer assessment: Effects of cognitive and affective feedback. *Instructional Science, 40*(2), 257–275.

Luckin, R., Holmes, W., Griffiths, M., & Pearson, L. B. F. (2016). *Intelligence Unsleashed. An argument for AI in Education. Pearson* (p. 57). Retrieved from http://oro.open.ac.uk/50104/1/Luckin et al. - 2016 - Intelligence Unleashed. An argument for AI in Educ.pdf%0Ahttps://static.googleusercontent.com/media/edu.google.com/pt-BR//pdfs/Intelligence-Unleashed-Publication.pdf

Malone, T. W., Laubacher, R., & Dellarocas, C. (2010, September). The collective intelligence genome. *IEEE Engineering Management Review.* https://doi.org/10.1109/EMR.2010.5559142

McGee, P., & Reis, A. (2012). Blended course design: A synthesis of best practices. *Journal of Asynchronous Learning Network, 16*(4), 7–22. https://doi.org/10.24059/olj.v16i4.239

McKinsey. (2008). Enduring Ideas: The 7-S Framework. *McKinsey Quarterly*, (March), 1–2. Retrieved from https://www.mckinsey.com/business-functions/strategy-and-corporate-finance/our-insights/enduring-ideas-the-7-s-framework http://www.mckinsey.com/insights/strategy/enduring_ideas_the_7-s_framework

Mento, A., Martinelli, P., and Jones, R. (1999), "Mind mapping in executive education: applications and outcomes," *Journal of Management Development, 18*(4), pp. 390–416.

Merleau-Ponty, M. (1964). *Child psychology and pedagogy The Sorbonne Lectures 1949-1952. Northwestern University studies in phenomenology and existential philosophy* (pp. xix, 505 s.).

Merriam, S. B. (2001). Andragogy and Self-Directed Learning: Pillars of Adult Learning Theory. *New Directions for Adult and Continuing Education, 2001*(89), 3. https://doi.org/10.1002/ace.3.

Merrill, D. (2007). Trends and Issues in Instructional Design and Technology, 2nd Edition. *Journal Trends and Issues in Instructional Design and Technology, 2,* 62–71.

Merrill, M. D. (2008). Converting e(subscript 3)-learning to e(superscript3)e-learning: An Alternative Instructional Design Method. In P. Shank & S. Carliner (Eds.), *The e-Learning Handbook: Past Promises, Present Challenges* (pp. 359–400). John Wiley& Sons, Incorporated. Retrieved from http://cito.byuh.edu/merrill/text/papers/e3 learning.pdf

Mezirow, J. (1991). *Transformative Dimensions of Adult Learning.* (J. Mezirow, Ed.), *The JosseyBass higher and adult education series* (p. 247). Jossey-Bass. Retrieved from http://eric.ed.gov/ERICWebPortal/recordDetail?accno=ED353469

National Reading Panel. (2000). Teaching children to read: An evidence-based assessment of the scientific research literature on reading and its implications for reading instruction. *NIH Publication No. 00-4769, 7,* 35. Retrieved from http://www.nichd.nih.gov/publications/nrp/upload/smallbook_pdf.pdf

Nesbit, J. C., & Adesope, O. O. (2013). Concept maps for learning. *Learning Through Visual Displays Gregory Schraw (Editor), Matthew T. McCrudden (Editor), Daniel Robinson (Editor)*, 303–328

O'Toole, S., & Essex, B. (2012). The adult learner may really be a neglected species. *Australian Journal of Adult Learning, 52*(1), 183–191

Owen, J. (2007). Program Evaluation: Forms and Approaches. *Evaluation and Program Planning, 30*(3), 320–321. Retrieved from http://linkinghub.elsevier.com/retrieve/pii/S0149718907000341

Plomp, T. (2013). Educational Design Research: A Introduction. In T. Plomp & N. Nieveen (Eds.), *Educational Design Research* (pp. 10–51). SLO. Retrieved from http://international.slo.nl/publications/edr/

Plomp, T., & Nieveen, N. (2009). References and Sources on Educational Design Research. In T. Plomp & N. Nieveen (Eds.), *An Introduction to Educational Design Research* (pp. 103–124). SLO: Netherlands Institute for Curriculum Development.

Reynolds, J., & Mason, R. (2016). Theories & Models Used for eLearning. *ELearning Fundamentals*, 1–9. Retrieved from http://books.google.ca/books?hl=en&lr=&id=Ao6jJqC6kiEC&oi=fnd&pg=PR6&dq=%22the+context+in+which+learning+occurs%22+%22blended+learning%22&ots=3sR1Klq2HM&sig=7gX0Sy0IMu4IaZwKsuXq8xCM97k.

Schunk, D. H. (2012). *Learning theories: An educational perspective.* (M. Harlan, Ed.), *Reading* (Vol. 5, p. 578). Pearson. Retrieved from http://www.amazon.com/Learning-Theories-Educational-Perspective-6th/dp/0137071957

Seels, B., & Glasgow, Z. (1998). Using Models and Paradigms. In *Making Instructional Design Decisions* (2ⁿᵈ ed., p. 342).

Singh, G., & Hardaker, G. (2017). Change levers for unifying top-down and bottom-up approaches to the adoption and diffusion of e-learning in higher education. *Teaching in Higher Education, 22*(6), 736–748. https://doi.org/10.1080/13562517.2017.1289508

Sotala, K. (2012). Advantages of artificial intelligences, uploads, and digital minds. *International Journal of Machine Consciousness, 4*(1), 275–291. https://doi.org/10.1142/S1793843012400161

Spector, J. M. (2014). Conceptualizing the emerging field of smart learning environments. *Smart Learning Environments, 1*(1). https://doi.org/10.1186/s40561-014-0002-7

Stanford University. (2017). An introduction to design thinking process guide. Hasso Plattner Institute of Design Stanford University website.

Steven H. Appelbaum, Sally Habashy, Jean-Luc Malo, & Hisham Shafiq. (2012). Back to the future: revisiting Kotter's 1996 change model Steven. *Journal of Management Development, 31*(8), 764–782. Hagel, J., Brown, J. S., and Davison, L. (2009). The big shift: Measuring the forces of change. *Harvard Business Review.* Harvard Business School Publishing.

Storberg-Walker, J. (2008). Wenger's Communities of Practice Revisited: A (Failed?) Exercise in Applied Communities of Practice Theory-Building Research. *Advances in Developing Human Resources, 10*(4), 555–577. https://doi.org/10.1177/1523422308319541

Cheung, S. K., Fong, R. W. tsz, Leung, S. K. Y., & Ling, E. K. wei. (2019). The Roles of Hong Kong Preservice Early Childhood Teachers' Creativity and Zest in Their Self-efficacy in

Creating Child-centered Learning Environments. *Early Education and Development, 30*(6), 788–799. https://doi.org /10.1080/10409289.2019.1586224

Sumara, D. J., & Davis, B. (1997). Enactivist theory and community learning: Toward a complexified understanding of action research. *Educational Action Research, 5*(3), 403–422. https:// doi.org/10.1080/09650799700200037

Taylor, E. W. (Mar 2007). An update of transformative learning theory: a critical review of the empirical research (1999–2005). *International Journal of Lifelong Education, 26* (2), 173–191.

Uljens, M. (2004). *School didactics and learning: A school didactic model framing an analysis of pedagogical implications of learning theory. School Didactics And Learning* (pp. 1–12). Psychology Press.

Walker, D. H. T., Bourne, L. M., & Shelley, A. (2008). Influence, stakeholder mapping and visualization. *Construction Management and Economics, 26*(6), 645–658. https://doi. org/10.1080/01446190701882390

Walker, D. H. T., Bourne, L. M., and Shelley, A. (2008). Influence, stakeholder mapping and visualization. Construction Management and Economics, 26(6), 645–658.

Wang, S. and Heffernan, N. (2009). Ethical issues in Computer-Assisted Language Learning: Perceptions of teachers and learners. British Journal of Educational Technology, vol. 41, no. 5, pp. 796–813, 2009.

Watson, J. B. (1913). Psychology as the behaviorist views it. Psychological Review, 20(2), 158–177.

Weld, D. S., Lin, C. H., and Bragg, J. (2014). Artificial Intelligence and Collective Intelligence. Handbook of Collective Intelligence.

Wenger, E. (1998). Community of Practice: a Brief Introduction. *Learning in Doing, 15*(4), 1–7. Retrieved from WORD: http://www.ewenger.com/theory/

Wertsch, J. V. (2012). *Mind as Action. Mind as Action* (pp. 1–216). Oxford University Press. https://doi.org/10.1093/acprof:oso/9780195117530.001.0001

White, J. L., & Altschuld, J. W. (2012). Understanding the "what should be condition" in needs assessment data. *Evaluation and Program Planning, 35*(1), 124–132. https://doi.org/10.1016/j.evalprogplan.2011.09.001

Wiggins, G. P. (1993). *The Jossey-Bass education series. Assessing student performance: Exploring the purpose and limits of testing.* Jossey-Bass.

Wolters, C. A. (2004). Advancing achievement goal theory: Using goal structures and goal orientations to predict students' motivation, cognition, and achievement. *Journal of Educational Psychology, 96*(2), 236–250. https://doi.org/10.1037/0022-0663.96.2.236

Woolf, B. P., Lane, H. C., Chaudhri, V. K., & Kolodner, J. L. (2013). AI grand challenges for education. *AI Magazine, 34*(4), 66–84. https://doi.org/10.1609/aimag.v34i4.2490

Yadin, A. (2013). Soft Systems Methodology in an Educational Context—Enhancing Students Perception and Understanding. *International Journal of E-Education, e-Business, e-Management and e-Learning.* https://doi.org/10.7763/ijeeee.2013.v3.258

Yampolskiy, R. V., & Fox, J. (2012). Artificial General Intelligence and the Human Mental Model (pp. 129–145). https://doi.org/10.1007/978-3-642-32560-1_7

Zainuddin, Z., Habiburrahim, H., & Hermawan, H. D. (2018). Designing a Technology-Enhanced Flipped Learning Model Using Schoology LMS. In *Proceeding - 2018 International Seminar on Intelligent Technology and Its Application, ISITIA 2018* (pp. 245–250). Institute of Electrical and Electronics Engineers Inc. https://doi.org/10.1109/ISITIA.2018.8710778

Zholdasbekov, A. A., Sikhynbayeva, Z. S., Zholdasbekova, B. A., Lekerova, G. Z., & Orasov, S. B. (2014). Psychological and pedagogical bases of active teaching methods. *Life Science Journal, 11*(SPEC. ISSUE 6), 150–154.

Zhu, Z., Yu, M., and Riezebos, P. A. (2016). Research Framework of Smart Education. Smart Learn. Environ. 3, 4 (2016). doi:10.1186/s40561-016-0026-2